Bishop T. D. Jakes, preacher, author, motivator and entrepreneur, one of the most respected and influential voices in the country today. Now, in *The Great Investment*, Bishop Jakes gives readers the blueprint for balanced successful living. He explains how the triad of faith, family and finance is the cornerstone of a life of moral success—success based on God's plan.

FAITH is the foundation of all that we want to achieve. Bishop Jakes explores the impact faith can have in healing and restoring quality of life to those whose history has caused them setbacks.

FAMILY is the anchor, keeping us grounded, supporting us, and allowing us to stay focused. A healthy family sustains us while giving meaning to our endeavors.

Finally, and no less crucial, FINANCE is the often misunderstood factor in the equation for success. Bishop Jakes removes the veil from this frequently neglected topic, and shows that not only is it not profane to focus on this area, it is essential.

Bishop T. D. Jakes's goal is to empower every woman and man. With this new book he provides the tools for us to chart a course for success and accomplish everything that God has promised. This is truly a book of our time.

continued...

PRAISE FOR OTHER BOOKS BY

T. D. JAKES

The Lady, Her Lover, and Her Lord

"A groundbreaking book . . . Jakes argues that high aspirations and achievements are not incompatible with love, marriage and sacred duty."

—*People*

"If you want to know the secret to a fulfilling life as a lady, if you want to know how to strengthen your relationship with your love, and most of all, if you want to establish a stronger fellowship with your Lord, then this book is for you. Bishop T. D. Jakes is a breath of fresh air. . . . Take it from me, the material within this book does make a difference."

—Natalie Cole

"[Jakes] demonstrates an unusual ability to inspire, uplift, teach and comfort. An eloquent wordsmith . . . [he] writes with an abundance of memorable metaphors and yet speaks to women's hearts in practical, often humorous terms . . . this masterful preacher offers all women sound advice and gentle, respectful encouragement."

—*Publishers Weekly*

Maximize the Moment

"To me, there is no man of God who is more gifted, more compassionate, more articulate, more anointed to reach and touch lives, small and great, than T. D. Jakes."

—Oral Roberts

"[A] handbook for reaching one's full potential. . . . You'll want to read this one."

—*Fort Worth Star-Telegram*

ALSO BY T. D. JAKES

Maximize the Moment

The Lady, Her Lover and Her Lord

His Lady

The GREAT Investment

Faith, Family and Finance

T. D. JAKES

B

BERKLEY BOOKS, NEW YORK

This publication is designed to provide accurate and authoritative information in regard to the subject matter covered. It is sold with the understanding that the publisher is not engaged in rendering legal, accounting, or other professional services. If you require legal advice or other expert assistance, you should seek the services of a competent professional.

Scripture quotations noted NIV are from The Holy Bible, New International Version. Copyright 1973, 1978, 1984 by International Bible Society. Used by permission of Zondervan Publishing House. All rights reserved.

Scripture quotations noted NKJV are from the New King James Version of the Bible. Copyright 1979, 1980, 1982, Thomas Nelson, Inc., Publishers.

Scripture quotations noted NASB are taken from the Holy Bible, New American Standard Version. Copyright The Lockman Foundation, 1960, 1962, 1963, 1968, 1971, 1972, 1973, 1975, 1977. Used by permission. Scripture quotations marked NLT are from The Holy Bible, New Living Translation. Copyright 1996. Used by permission of Tyndale House Publishers, Inc., Wheaton, Illinois 60189. All rights reserved.

A Berkley Book
Published by The Berkley Publishing Group
A division of Penguin Putnam Inc.
375 Hudson Street
New York, New York 10014

Copyright © 2000 by T. D. Jakes.
Cover design copyright © 2000 by Walter Harper.
Text design by Jennifer Ann Daddio.

All rights reserved.
This book, or parts thereof, may not be reproduced
in any form without permission.
BERKLEY and the "B" design are trademarks belonging to
Penguin Putnam Inc.

PRINTING HISTORY

G. P. Putnam's Sons hardcover edition / November 2000
Berkley trade paperback edition / March 2002

Berkley trade paperback ISBN: 0-425-18345-9

Visit our website at
www.penguinputnam.com

The Library of Congress has catalogued the G. P. Putnam's Sons hardcover edition as follows:

Jakes, T. D.
The great investment : faith, family and finance / T. D. Jakes.
p.   cm.
ISBN 0-399-14683-0
1. Christian life.   2. Family—Religious aspects—Christianity.   3. Finance,
Personal—Religious aspects—Christianity.   I. Title.
BV4501.2.J333   2000   00-062671
248.4—dc21

PRINTED IN THE UNITED STATES OF AMERICA

10   9   8   7   6   5   4   3   2   1

Most Berkley Books are available at special quantity discounts for bulk purchases for sales promotions, premiums, fund-raising, or educational use. Special books, or book excerpts, can also be created to fit specific needs.

For details, write: Special Markets, The Berkley Publishing Group, 375 Hudson Street, New York, New York 10014.

Acknowledgments

There are many people who invested in the development of this project who must be, and should be, acknowledged. Without them I would not have been able to meet the stringent demands of my life and still provide the quality information that was essential to this kind of project. Their investment in me makes it possible for me to invest my message and thoughts in you.

My gratitude to my family, who generously shared me with this manuscript. I will always appreciate your love and support. I also want to acknowledge the compassion and encouragement that I consistently received from my church family.

Thank you to Denise Silvestro, who tirelessly labored to enhance this project with her insights and creativity. Her grace to race as we edited and developed this book was a significant component in reaching the deadline to get this timely message out to the people who needed it most.

Thank you, Joel Fotinos, for your enthusiasm, encouragement, wisdom, and for believing in my message and my method.

Thanks also to A. Larry Ross and Associates, who helped to manage my schedule and protect my interests in countless ways.

I deeply appreciate David Yeazell, who tirelessly worked with me in developing and assisting in the conveyance and structure of the truths contained in this new book. I also want to thank Eli Dragon, who began the laborious task of making me more investment literate.

Thank you to everyone at Putnam. You all treated me and my work with great dignity and integrity. My gratitude to Phyllis Grann, Susan Petersen Kennedy, Marilyn Ducksworth, Dan Harvey, Dick Heffernan, Martha Bushko, and everyone at JMS Marketing & Sales, Inc.

There are several people I would like to dedicate this book to:

To Mrs. Minerva Coles, who let an eight-year-old boy named Tommy Jakes cut her grass, and although I probably scalped her yard, she gave me an eight-dollar check, which I framed and hung in my room for fifteen years or more. Mrs. Coles gave me my first taste of employment and fueled my entrepreneurial drive.

To Brownie Bartlett from Union Carbide, who demanded that I learn how to stick to a job I hated.

To my mother (deceased), who drove her car through the snow to help me deliver newspapers and collect weekly from the neighbors in my community.

To my father (also deceased), who gave me the job of wrapping smelly fresh fish in newspaper. He sold "fresh" fish out of the back of his red pickup truck so that he could buy groceries for his family. He taught me the value of hard work. All I am and ever will be is in tribute, triumph, and declaration to a man and his wife who persevered in the face of the many obstacles of the times and brought not only bread to the house but values and dreams to the soul.

To Mrs. Virginia Jamison, my wife's mother and my friend, who cried over my first real honorarium and dressed our kids in the winter when I was struggling.

Oh, and speaking of the struggle, I would also like to dedicate this book to my lovely wife, Serita Ann Jakes, who has been the compass that gives me direction in the sea of choices that have always surrounded my career and life. I dedicate this book to my wife and our children because they knew me when our family faced frailty, our finances were incredibly weak, and my faith in myself and in God was definitely on trial. Only they and a few close friends remember how we struggled and fought our way up after the plant closed, and how we survived unemployment, applied for welfare for a brief period, and had our car repossessed. We lost everything but our faith, which paid off in spades!

To my dear wife, who boiled bath water for me on an electric range when the gas was disconnected. Who created meals from nothing and never once complained. Who dressed the bleeding hands I had from digging ditches and lifted my bruised ego the first time I had to go get milk from the WIK program. It is from our life together that I extract the nuggets of wisdom that will hopefully empower others to run on broken legs, crawl on crushed knees, and stand on twisted feet. Thanks for believing in me. Together we have survived through the winds of life, burying our parents, raising our children, enduring the plights and plagues of being human while expected to be divine. It has not been easy.

But, if I had to fight through life a second time, I would still choose you as my partner. You are The Greatest Investment in which I have ever placed my stock!

Just one final note: This book is written not about God but to God Himself. It is He Who knows who I really am and Whose love has finally convinced me that it doesn't matter. His grace is greater than my stumbling, stammering humanity. I have always been strong in some places and frail in others, sure about one thing while worried about another. In spite of my weaknesses, You comforted and blessed me. Blessing me was like painting a Picasso on inexpensive canvass. You do Your best work with inferior materials.

When You did decide it was time to bless me—boy, did You ever! I am certain that whatever I have accomplished was simply a matter of Your divine favor. You are the best financial advisor, secret-keeper, family counselor, emotional stabilizing influence I have ever met. Thanks for giving me tips on stocks, bonds, annuities, people, and places and things. I have profited in every area through knowing You as my Lord.

My faith in You is fixed, my faith in me is growing, and my gratitude is too overwhelming to articulate in such a small span of life and with my limited linguistic artistry. To attempt to express my feelings for You is an intimidating undertaking. Exasperated by the efforts, I will succumb to slang to convey the depth of my love, gratitude, and undying devotion. Although it is simply stated, it is nonetheless of profound significance to me. As my children would say, so say I: Heavenly Father, You de Man!

Contents

Introduction   *1*

PART ONE: FINANCE

1. From One Extreme: Poverty   9

2. To the Other Extreme: Abundance   19

3. The Power to Get Wealth   33

4. The Power of Compounding   49

5. A Plan to Get Wealth   63

PART TWO: FAMILY

6. Family Matters   79

7. Intimacy Means Into-me-see   95

8. My Family Is My Team   107

9. Help, My House Is Out of Control   125

PART THREE: FAITH

10. Faith, the Compass of My Soul   143

11. Without a Touch   159

12. Faith Develops in the Dark!   177

13. Evidence That Demands a Verdict   191

Final Words   207

Introduction

Isn't it interesting how so many things come in threes? There are three aspects of God—Father, Son, and Holy Spirit. There are three parts of man—body, mind, and soul. There are three stages of life—eternity past, eternity present, and eternity future. The Pauline epistles refer to a group of three as well; Paul writes of faith, hope, and charity. The Hebrew chronologist speaks of the inner court, the outer court, and the holiest of holies. Even our government breaks down into three branches: the executive, the judicial, and the legislative, all three working together to form a system in which justice is served.

In this book I present to you another group of three—three aspects that are essential to the life traveler in order to be happy and successful on this journey. We can carry only a limited number of bags if we are to move efficiently and effectively to our desired destination. Too much baggage and we get weighted down, caught up in the minutiae of a mundane existence. However, too little and we lack the necessities to sustain us on our trip. I believe that there are three bags we should all carry: faith for the hard times; family for the fulfillment of intimate and interpersonal needs; and finances through which one acquires the luxury of options. Faith, family, and finance—a threefold cord that is not easily broken. If you can carry these three and not destroy one in the pursuit of another, nothing is impossible to achieve. Just three things for a lifelong trip, but what a powerful three they are.

Faith is that indescribable strength, that secret weapon of the soul, which allows us to persevere even when the facts seem damning and the truth unbearable. It is what keeps us going when travel conditions are unfavorable and we're not sure we can continue. It is the light that leads us out of the darkness and the map that guides our way. Without faith, we would likely pull over on the side of the road, give up, and watch everyone else pass us by.

Sometimes faith seems in short supply. When faced with adversity and hard times, we may have a tendency to turn our backs and deny God's glory. But it is at these very times when we need our faith the most. When we trust in the Lord and believe with utmost confidence that He will guide us, there is nothing we cannot withstand and walk through. Realize that faith is like a muscle; trouble and opposition may strain it, but in the end it will grow stronger.

Also essential to a successful journey is the solid support of a loving and nurturing family. Unfortunately, in this day and age, this is a scarce commodity. But let's stop for a moment and define family. Certainly it is mother and father, sister and brother, spouse and child. But it also encompasses aunts and uncles, grandparents, godparents, distant relatives, and close friends. When I speak of family, I mean those whose arms have held you, whose words have lifted you, and whose values have kept you rooted. We need the unconditional love and understanding of family—whether that be birth family, adopted family, or even church family. We equally require the legacy of values and dreams passed down from our parents, grandparents, and their grandparents before them. We need the anchor that our community and our cultural family provide as well.

But family, in whatever form, needs strategic planning, unfaltering commitment, and concerted effort. In this book I will discuss the investment required versus the returns expected. We all want the return, but we do not always realize that there is an investment required. The second issue is that the investment may be long term. Your family will pay you back, but often over decades, not weeks, months, or even years. It is a long-term investment with quite a bit of inequities along the way. However, eventually you will reap a return on your investment. It may come in one moment of need, during a crisis, or it may trickle out in little "be there" moments that are significant to you. But you will reap only what you have sown. So let the long, laborious process of sowing begin. Every season we miss is a cycle we lose, and every cycle we lose is a harvest delayed.

Perhaps the most important item for many who will read this book is the frank and open discussion about finances. Finance has for so long been a taboo subject among people of faith. For some, a focus on piety has caused them to lag behind. They are taught that money is the root of all evil and should thus be forsaken. But every dream needs financing. Every talent needs a stage. Every message needs a method of conveyance. Ideas die without the funds to realize them. As Christians, we have a great message and a wonderful philosophy of living; they should not be muted by a lack of financial dexterity.

There are others who get caught up in the material world and equate wealth with strength of faith. They believe that God's blessings can be counted in dollars and cents, and one's financial status is an indication of one's status in the eyes of the Lord. They begin pursuing money for money's sake. Material goods become their gods, and banks become their churches. They lose sight of the fact that although God does indeed bless us with financial success, we should be mindful to worship the Giver and not the gift.

In this book I set out to balance the extreme teachings of the Church. I seek to find the equilibrium between the monastic philosophy of frugalness and the obsessive pursuit of wealth as a means of displaying one's spirituality. I want to address the issues of investing and help you develop a plan that will enable you to benefit from the gifts that God wants to give you. Practical matters coupled with faithfulness to God and His word will unlock the blessing of the Lord. We must learn to combine faith with works.

So now we begin to knit together the threefold cord of faith, family, and finance. The garment that we knit today is one that is designed to insulate us from the cold chill of regret and despair that comes when one fails to maximize his or her moments and misses the opportunities to invest in life. Yes, all of life is an investment. Where there is great investment, there will be great return. Where there is little investment, there is little return. Life doesn't afford us the opportunity to pay what we like and still gain what we want. We need to invest today so that we can reap the rewards tomorrow. We must be like the ants and prepare for tomorrow today. I know a lot of people who failed to be like the ants, and in the winter of their lives were depressed and resentful, cursing their wasted youth. They didn't invest in the future and later in life found themselves in a financial, emotional, and spiritual state of poverty. They died poor, bitter, and complaining for lack of an invested life's plan.

> Go to the ant, you sluggard; consider its ways and be wise! It has no commander, no overseer or ruler, yet it stores its provisions in summer and gathers its food at harvest. How long will you lie there, you sluggard? When will you get up from your sleep? A little sleep, a little slumber, a little folding of the hands to rest—and poverty will come on you like a bandit and scarcity like an armed man.
>
> PROVERBS 6:6–11 (NIV)

The ants are preparing, the birds are building their nests, the beaver is constructing his dam. All of creation invests in the future, prepares for the winter, and delays gratification for the purpose of a better tomorrow. We should follow their lead and begin to set our sights on tomorrow while maximizing our moments today. We need to invest in faith, family, and finance, and let these three form the foundation of all our success.

Ain't Life a Trip

Fasten your seat belts. We're traveling through this world at a breakneck speed. Life passes quickly and we need to make the most of our journey. Make sure you are carrying what you need and have a travel plan to get where you're going. Maximize every moment, but don't fail to invest in the future. I challenge the faithful to be practical. I charge the practical to be faithful. One must complement the other. I encourage you all to nurture your family and impart to them the wisdom, values, and goals you accrue over your lifetime.

Onward, fellow travelers! Godspeed! Take this humble offering, the sum of my life experience thus far. Use this advice to set a course for your future, formulate a strategy to carry it out, and gain the strength and inspiration to see it through. Dare to dream and aim for goals far beyond your current position. Seek to move ahead and reach heights unimagined. Keep your sights set on the future and be ever mindful of the legacy you leave behind. Are you ready to take off? Prepare for the journey, expect the unexpected, and enjoy the trip!

One thing is certain: You have a day to be born and a day to die, and in between you have the greatest investment you will ever make. You invest your time, your strength, your youth, and ultimately, like Christ, you are laying your life down in your business, in your relationships, and in your church. Every day that passes is a day spent, a day you will never see again. You cannot stop the spending process. But you can control where you spend your days, with whom you spend them, and what you spend them on. You want the most beneficial return on every day spent, don't you? Then make the Great Investment in the big three—faith, family, and finance—and have the time of your life!

Part One

FINANCE

1.

From One Extreme: Poverty

I have experienced success and struggle, power and poverty. I have thrived and been thwarted by a fluctuating economy. I have lived on both sides of the track, and my shoes have walked down shantytown streets and sidewalks paved with gold. I know that hard work and determination can overcome humble beginnings, and that circumstances beyond our control can tumble fortunes like a house of cards. For some, success was handed to them as they were born into wealthy families and were given choices and opportunities denied to most. I have seen people go from wealth to gross poverty through one bad business decision, one prolonged illness, a lawsuit, a problem child. Success is fragile.

I have traveled to various regions and experienced many diverse cultures. I have observed certain communities that resented success and have come into contact with others that catered to its magical charms as if it were the end-all destination in life to be rich. Yet regardless of viewpoint, I have noticed a common tendency to have disdain for those on a different socioeconomic level. We often shun others whose life circumstances remind us that ours could have been different. Rich and poor alike develop a fraternity that denies membership to people whose financial status is different from their own.

> Accept responsibility for your financial future.

One would think that the faith community would be the one place where all could find access without fear of rejection, but unfortunately that is not the reality. In fact, the status and wealth of parishioners has been an ongoing conflict in the thoughts of the church for years. Sadly, many have walked away from the faith of their childhood, finding it limiting and inflexible. Often it is not the faith that they resent but the financial climate of that community of faith that conflicts with their own goals, values, and objectives.

I have watched with great fascination as the church has moved from fad to fad and from phase to phase. In the process we have often gone from one extreme to the other, disregarding the significance of balance. Balance is a difficult thing to attain. Yet balance and prosperity go hand in hand. No one would last long in business if they never balanced their accounts or checkbook. Yet we often fail to balance our thinking and have found ourselves with insufficiencies because of dangerous extremes.

Monastic Frugalness

One need only look over the shoulder of the church to see that we have come through many eras of growth to arrive at this juncture of the twenty-first century. Glance in the rearview mirror of church history and you will see somewhere in the depths of the Middle Ages, in a musty, monastic cell, a robed monk knelt in prayer. His gnarled, leathery hands are clenched tightly as he recites the evening prayers that have graced the end of each day from the time he first took his vows and stepped foot in the community that became his family, and continued as such until the expiration of his life on earth.

Like many before him and many after him, he aspired to a higher degree of spirituality than was available to the laity, who were bound to carnal pleasures and material acquisitions. His trek to godliness led him into a life of vows—vows taken to separate him from the world and its influences. They were vows of chastity and poverty. He would never marry nor touch a woman, and would never own property other than the brown, worn cloak on his back and the tattered prayer book beside his bed. His denial of physical pleasures was motivated by the idea that the things of the world were a passing evil and in direct opposition to the things of the spirit of God. Thus, if one wanted to attain a more spiritual life, he had to separate himself from the temporal, deny the flesh, and turn to a life of long prayers, hard work, and frugal living.

This quest for God, while admirable, denied those who pursued it even the legitimate pleasures of marriage and family. Good men denied reproduction while madmen produced child after child. The wealth was left in the hands of the wicked, whereas the Bible plainly says that the wealth of the unjust should be laid up for

> *God blesses the actions of men and women who are not afraid to make a move.*

the just. These well-intentioned men thought self-denial would allow them an indifference to the world around them, as they awaited a better world tomorrow. They did not realize that we are sent here to affect the world we are in while we wait on the world to come. Whoever writes the check controls the flow. Economy and effectiveness are comrades in society. Economy rules the globe more than morality. Whether we approve of it or not, the financial climate has global impact and personal ramifications.

The monastic frugalness philosophy served a purpose for the rich and the poor. It allowed the once self-indulgent convert to do penance for his or her own sins by self-denial. It comforted those who had never had financial freedom with the privilege of demonizing the unattainable fruit as the forbidden fruit. It was simple to them: Money was evil, happiness was evil; God wants us frugal and self-flagellating. It glorified works of men to pay the debt of sin. But the truth is this is a debt that God alone can pay.

A Worldwide Tradition

The monastic tradition of denial of the flesh is seen throughout history, in virtually every religious tradition and every group of people on the planet. Christianity is not the only world religion to place frugalness on a level with godliness. Buddhism and Hinduism, among others, have a long history of religious asceticism. The more you could separate yourself from the material world, and get rid of the desire for the sensual pleasures of the world

> *Current assets should be approximately two times greater than current liabilities.*

(things that looked good, smelled good, tasted good, felt good, and sounded good), the quicker you could attain to a higher spiritual level. In fact, in many traditions it was considered an honor for a son to devote himself to a monastic lifestyle, in hopes that the prayers and sacrifice of the son would somehow bless and atone for the family left dealing with the carnal muck of marriage and raising children and making money and putting food on the table.

Unfortunately, poverty as equated with godliness is one extreme in the Christian's view on wealth, and sadly there are those today whose theology is still affected by this extreme thinking. Historically, it is easy to identify the monastic frugalness of certain streams in the broad river called Christianity. It is also easy to criticize the tenets that led to the priest being celibate and poor for life. But the reality is that this same philosophy moved from the hallowed walls of monasteries into the country churches on backwoods roads of farming towns across America. It crept into the tambourine-beating services of storefront churches in the 1950s and '60s. It was a message sailing on the winds of the Depression, thirty years before but still palpable to the poor who didn't rebound from the hard times. This message demonized success in a manner that helped to comfort the impoverished with the hope of heaven. It suggested that current suffering was a small price to pay for the luxury of the sweet by and by. It almost intimated that future bliss was being paid for by the emptiness of the present. All that was humorous, enjoyable, and entertaining

The gifts God has given you are enough to bring you before great men.

was considered demonic, including television, the circus, and dancing. All emblems of outward success were renounced. Jewelry was out of the question, but no one could afford it anyway. Fine clothes were considered a sign of vanity, but who would be fool enough to spend their meager livelihood on suits and silk dresses when they had a house full of children to feed and bills to pay?

You see, the old saints who taught us back then had nothing, so it only seemed right to preach that having things was of the devil and that those who had things were living opulent lives now but were going to burn in hell for that success. Deep in the psyches of those old-time believers was the sense of satisfaction that their lack brought them closer to God. Not having things put them on a higher plane than those who did. They sang with sincerity the verse "I'd rather have Jesus than silver and gold, I'd rather be his than have riches untold . . ." A true believer was not like the High Church type who worshiped in cathedrals and wore furs and lived high off the hog. A true believer, and true faith, was simple and quaint. True believers worshiped in clapboard meetinghouses or downtown storefronts, and more often than not lived down with the hogs. These were devout Christians who meant well. They were only trying to insulate themselves from the pain of want and desire. This was the Holiness movement, strong in spirit but often weak in theology. And although those who embraced this philosophy did have a strong spiritual life, their influence in this world was weak.

> *Jealousy over others' success kills your own creativity and dampens your influence.*

14

The Depression passed, times changed, but these people didn't. The world evolved, but they remained steeped in antiquated concepts that were reflective of slavery and poverty. The global economy took a step forward, but they lagged behind. Yes, many didn't have the means to take advantage of all the opportunities that world offered, but it was their sluggish mentality that kept them shackled to the past and their poverty. With better education and an embracing of the changes around them, they could have, if not kept up, at least stayed in the race. Sadly, they turned their backs on progress and demonized success. How much more impact these good Christians could have had if only they availed themselves of the riches the world offered.

Don't get the wrong idea—poverty can build character. I learned much about God's love for me and His ability to faithfully provide daily bread for my family through poverty. But the scripture that speaks of never seeing the righteous forsaken or their seed begging bread (Psalms 37:25) does not tell us how bad it has to get before the righteous would be labeled as being forsaken. It only tells us that they would not be forsaken.

My whole definition of poverty was changed as I started to travel around America and visit Third World countries. As you walk the dusty roads of South Africa or fan the flies away from your brow in Jamaica, you realize that we have little sense of real poverty. When you see your American brothers and sisters sleeping in the streets and eating out of garbage cans, you understand what it means to "do without." Around the world there are many righteous people

> *A budget can bring focus to your financial affairs.*

who are going to bed hungry. Their sustenance is meager and gives them a minimal allowance of vitamins and minerals. And, amazingly, although they are not full, they are not forsaken. "Give us this day our daily bread" is a daily prayer request for food, something fully understood only by someone who doesn't know where his or her next meal is coming from. Yet even in the most extreme cases of impoverishment there is still a knowing in many of them that somehow or another God still provides. Their meager fare doesn't at all indicate there is a lack of faith, as some have suggested. It is their faith that allows many of them to survive the tempestuously painful realities of their existence.

Many are the prophets whose powerful ministry called down fire and yet they were financially challenged for a season. In spite of their lack, they remained faithful to God. For them, as for many of us, poverty builds character in trusting God. I have often commented to my wife that we give our children everything except what made us strong—in other words, a struggle. It is in the furnace of affliction that faith shines brightly. The white heat of an unquenchable faith burns with passion in the hearts of people who have believed God *in spite of,* as opposed to those who believe God *because of.* The furnace polishes faith. No, we don't want to go through it. But if we must, we find praise in the midst of pain. There is a grace to endure hardships that reveals God.

But please understand that doesn't mean we should seek calamity; we shouldn't create a crisis for God to resolve. This would be like when Satan tested Jesus in the wilderness (Matthew 4:1–11). We don't need to test God. Often people do not maximize themselves, supposing that God will do it for them. But the adage "God helps those who help themselves" is true. He has gifted you with the abilities, but it is up to you to exercise them.

There are others who think that they will get "extra credit" for being self-degrading. No, this is not the way. We don't drink poison because we like the taste of the antidote. If life has, through no fault of our own, landed us in a crisis situation, we know that He is the Christ over the crises. But just because one experiences God in poverty does not mean that poverty is godliness.

2.

To the Other Extreme: Abundance

Faith and finances have become the wonder twins of the twenty-first century. True faith can be seen in success as well as struggle, but unfortunately there is a belief among some Christians that the strength of a man's faith is demonstrated by the abundance of his possessions. In an often sincere, well-meaning effort to raise the standard of the impoverished, there has been placed on them a sense of shame, as if there is some great wrong they did that accounts for their present circumstances. They then spend their last penny trying to give enough to God to convince Him to break some supposed curse. The danger of this counsel is strangely similar to that of Job's friends who counseled him that his sickness and poverty were somehow his fault. Time proved them to be faulty in their judgment and lacking in true discernment. We can't condemn those who have fallen on hardships.

In this chapter we will explore the idea that giving and receiving, seedtime and harvest are valid principles that, if acted out properly, will bring prosperity. I agree with these precious biblical truths. But I want to clearly say that many have relied on the principles of sowing and reaping without any regard for balancing their faith with works. You need good Christianity with good credit. It is important that we do not allow people to reach over the practical for the spectacular. Even in the wilderness, Israel was fed by God through spectacular means only when there was not opportunity to do it through practical means.

Know where your money is going; keep accurate records of all spending.

I want you to implement the spectacular advantage of your faith while benefiting from the practical principles of better business, banking, and financial planning. Financial health is important, and a valid topic among Christians. We should not bury our heads in the sand and passively wait for our just rewards. But nor should we dedicate our lives to the acquisition of riches and material goods. Ultimately our goal as believers should not be how wealthy we can be but how well we can be. Wealth and well-being are not always synonymous. Remember, balance is the goal we are ardently pursuing.

Wealth As Godliness

Sometime in the late twentieth century, in a North American church, a finely attired, golden-haired preacher paces the wide expanse of his sanctuary's altar. His clenched grip wrinkles the pages of his black, leather-bound King James Bible with annotations and footnotes and Holy Land maps in the back. His church is lavishly decorated with plush carpets, silk floral arrangements, and the finest religious articles and furniture available. Everything about the place is opulent, from marble columns to valet parking. Only the best for this church and preacher. Unlike his monastic brother, this man has not taken vows of chastity or poverty. To the contrary, he has purposely pursued success and prosperity. His gospel is pure gold. Sure, good news to the poor is a part of the Gospel, but it is not all of it. His success does not offend me if it ultimately leads others to a deeper and richer life, if he mentors others spiritually and economically.

> The Spirit of the Sovereign LORD is on me, because the LORD has anointed me to preach good news to the poor. He has sent me to bind up the brokenhearted, to proclaim freedom for the captives and release from darkness for the prisoners, to proclaim the year of the LORD's favor and the day of vengeance of our God, to comfort all who mourn, and provide for those who grieve in Zion—to bestow on them a crown of beauty instead of ashes, the oil of gladness instead of mourning, and a garment of praise instead of a spirit of despair.
>
> ISAIAH 61:1–3 (NIV)

Is our preacher friend wrong to teach the poor about the blessings of God? No, of course not. It is a part of the message, but it is not the entire message. He has forgotten the teachings of salvation and the cross and discarded them as not being progressive. He is primarily interested in

> *Save receipts from all transactions and record amounts in a budget log.*

how much he can grasp in the here and now. He is a far cry from the monastery we just left. He is married; his wife and children are stretched out in the first row of the upholstered oak pews. He owns more than the cloak on his back. In fact, he owns two homes, three cars, and a brand-new boat. He'd rather have Jesus *and* silver and gold and riches untold. His message is simple: You can have what you want; God will give it to you; all you must do

> *Always expect, ask for, and get a receipt.*

is name it, ask for it, and from this moment forth claim what it is already yours. You want a new Cadillac, say so by faith. You'd like a bigger house, ask for it by faith. You want to have a bigger bank account, claim it by faith. If you only had enough faith, you could have it all, he spouts from his lofty position on his gilded pulpit. He has lost touch with the true meaning of the riches the Lord has promised us and has lost compassion in the process. He condemns the poor and believes that they don't have enough because they don't give enough. He and his kind preach that poverty is a result of sin, so if you are poor you lack faith and are obviously living on a lower spiritual plane than those folk in the church who have more stuff than you.

Sadly, like the shepherd so go the sheep. Many who live their lives under this worldview see wealth as a sign of godliness. They believe their identity and acceptance by God is seen in the acquisition of things. The more you have, the more spiritual you must be and thus the more God must love you. You have a bigger car than I do, so you must have more faith. Poverty or apparent lack is seen as a lack of faith or the outright fruit of sin. Many in this camp live above their means to appear spiritual. The pressure to impress is driving them. The spirit is not leading them. They desperately want the look of success.

Let me emphasize: I don't think success is bad. I wish all of you success and prosperity. But you need to understand that as God blesses you, there is a greater and greater need to be a good steward. Stewardship is more than making offerings at church. It also includes a financial portfolio and estate planning that allows you to have the greatest impact with what God has given you. It is a tragic misappropriation of God's blessing when those who acquire wealth begin to drive luxury cars but drive home to trailers or cheap efficiency apartments at night. It is poor stewardship that causes a man to wear expensive watches, sport Gucci bags, and flash diamond rings but then fail to pay child support. Many spend hundreds of dollars on the latest imported suit and fine-skin shoes, only to struggle to scrape together the money needed to keep the lights from being cut off or the eviction notice from being delivered.

The pressure to impress has crept into the Church, and with it a teaching that discusses only economic empowerment without teaching how to administrate what God has empowered you to acquire. Obsessed with the need to impress, we are failing to learn how to be truly blessed. We are failing to learn the business skills for sustaining success and the spiritual skills that keep it all in perspective.

I say, stop the madness! Neither the

> *A budget is not to restrict you from enjoying life, but it is a tool to help you focus your finances on those goals that will allow you to lead a fulfilling life.*

make of your car nor the label in your clothes determines the faith in your heart. Your new cell phone, DVD player, or whatever latest status symbol you have doesn't represent your status in the eyes of the Lord. You can't buy your way into Heaven. Salvation is free.

Do I believe in supernatural return on your giving? Yes, sir! Do I believe God blesses tithes and offering? Yes, I do. But why should we teach you to claim a car without teaching you about the car payment and interest rates on the loan? Why should we encourage you to invest in items that depreciate—cars, clothes, and the latest technological advances that are outdated tomorrow— while you fail to invest in things that will appreciate with time? Why should we tell you about prosperity without helping you to develop a strategy that will bridge the gulf between what you believe and what you receive? It matters to me that we have taught people to be insatiable in their appetites and have taught them how to receive in their faith what they cannot budget with their checkbooks.

> *Use the credit you have wisely. Don't spend up to your credit limit.*

If it is in God's design for you to receive more financially, He knows when and how to release it. God doesn't pour new wine into old skins. Old wineskins lack elasticity, and when the wine fills them, the skins burst. Likewise, as you become more successful, if you do not change your business habits you will not be able to stand the increase that God wants to release to his children. Let's stop and get these wineskins ready for the outpouring that our faith teachers have been teaching us about. If we do not, we will be like the people who hit the lottery and end up broke in a year or two. All that God has given will leak through the cracked wineskins of poor business skills. Those old skins of poor business habits will nullify all of that great teaching about faith. Many of us are being healed from bad habits that would waste the promised blessings that God desires to give if he were to release it into the old wineskins of financial improprieties and obsessive spending binges that are associated with the lack of teaching and temperance. We need the faith teaching, but we also need the practical pragmatic concepts of what to do when the blessing comes, what to do while the blessing tarries, and what to do when the blessing is denied. It will bridge the gap between what you can conceive and what you can administrate.

Rich Poverty

Now, while it is necessary to learn how to manage money and transact business, that should not be all we are about. You must tend to the business at hand, but first tend to the business of God. Don't be like the Laodician Christians whom Paul writes about. They are described as rich and increased with goods. They have great wealth, but they are still poor by God's definition. They are poor inwardly. Work has become their God. Many people today fall into this trap. They are successful in the work world but impoverished in their souls. They are too busy working to be thankful for the God who gave them the job. They have the car and the house, the annuity, the stocks and the bonds. But having had it all, they find that there is a void in their lives. Tragically, no one ministers to the affluent. They assume that if you are accomplished you are completed. But the reality is that many people can be publicly successful and privately complete failures.

Tragically, many people have allowed their persona to be a "work mule attitude" that keeps piling more and more on their shoulders to help mask the deeper emptiness that exists in their private lives. It is often quite difficult to meet the demands of success without allowing yourself to become controlled by your life, rather than you controlling your life. I strongly believe in a work ethic, but like the faith message, if we view only one truth without heeding other truths, we lose the balance that is essential to keep us from becoming obsessive. It is much like a child who eats a lot of one food group and none of the others. The food group he enjoys isn't bad, he just needs to have a balanced diet. In that same sense, it is important that you are not bingeing on work. Success taken to an extreme becomes a disorder.

Godliness with Contentment

But godliness with contentment is great gain. For we brought nothing into the world, and we can take nothing out of it. But if we have food and clothing, we will be content with that. People who want to get rich fall into temptation and a trap and into many foolish and harmful desires that plunge men into ruin and destruction. For the love of money is a root of all kinds of evil. Some people, eager for money, have wandered from the faith and pierced themselves with many griefs. But you, man of God, flee from all this, and pursue righteousness, godliness, faith, love, endurance and gentleness.

1 TIMOTHY 6:6–11 (NIV)

Verse 6 teaches us that godliness coupled with contentment is great gain. The word *gain* means profit. A profit is what is accrued when the transaction is over. When all is said and done, you want to profit from every stage and age of your life. Profit comes when the faithful are contented, not being led by the lust of success nor driven by the promise of wealth, but calmly assured that God knows the whens, the whos, and hows of blessing his people. Verse 7 assures us that nothing tangible is eternal. No matter what we have attained, none of it is transportable to where we are going. The things seen are temporal and the things not seen are eternal, and never the twain shall meet.

Verse 8 makes the distinction between needs and wants. This allows the indigenous person who lives in a hut in India to say, "Thank you, Lord," just like the mansion dweller in Hollywood. They both thank God for the basics of life. You can't want to say "thank you" until we have attained the latest and newest definition of success. It is wrong not to thank God for where you are and what you have right now. It clogs up the pipeline of future blessings with unthankfulness. Verse 9 is important. It does not speak against being rich. It speaks against the desire to be rich. Being rich is not the goal. If it is, it becomes the god you worship, and the methods by which you attain it will take you farther from the true God who freely gives us all things.

What, then, shall we say in response to this? If God is for us, who can be against us? He who did not spare his own Son, but gave him up for us all—how will he not also, along with him, graciously give us all things?

ROMANS 8:31–32 (NIV)

"I tell you the truth," Jesus replied, "no one who has left home or brothers or sisters or mother or father or children or fields for me and the gospel will fail to receive a hundred times as much in this present age (homes, brothers, sisters, mothers, children and fields— and with them, persecutions) and in the age to come, eternal life."

MARK 10:29–30 (NIV)

I want to prove that God is not against us being affluent. Through our sacrifice and giving, He honors with a hundredfold return. This return is not in Heaven; as Jesus plainly promised, a hundredfold return will be gained in this life! Why would I need a hundredfold return in Heaven? I need the return on my investment in this life while still recognizing that the greater wealth is still, as He so aptly puts it, eternal life. He has promised that to those who sacrifice for His divine purpose.

Notice that "persecution" is mentioned right in the middle of Jesus' promise. It is part of the package. Others tend to be jealous of those who are exceptional. They see a hundredfold return and resent it. They somehow associate others' success with their struggle, as if someone else's blessing is the reason they have not done better. It's ironic, but they may ostracize you for having the very thing they want.

Can you stand to be blessed? Blessed people always cause

controversy. I have never met anyone who was exceptional and didn't cause ripples in the pond of mediocrity. Jesus knew that a hundredfold return causes ripples. As the Bible warns, to him whom much is given, much is required. There are requirements associated with fame; there are requirements imposed on leaders, builders, and mountain climbers of faith. Hard work may end in success, but success will always lead to controversy and criticism.

Seek the Giver and Not the Gift

> *But you, man of God, flee from all this, and pursue righteousness, godliness, faith, love, endurance and gentleness.*
>
> 1 TIMOTHY 6:11 (NIV)

Verse 11 teaches what you are to pursue. It is the pursuit of God and His righteousness, faith, and love that allows the other things to come your way. In fact, Jesus said if you seek God first, "all these things shall be added unto you" (Matthew 6:33, KJV). God will take care of you. God will give you all things, as He did Solomon and many others. He does this when He knows it is not for the things He gives that you seek His face. Surely you can understand that. Who wants someone who is more interested in what you can give him or her than they are in loving you? You must worship the giver, not the gift.

The Root of All Evil?

For the love of money is the root of all evil: which while some coveted after, they have erred from the faith, and pierced themselves through with many sorrows.

1 TIMOTHY 6:10 (KJV)

Money is neither evil nor good. It is what you do with it that colors it with moral relativity. The same hundred-dollar bill can feed a crack habit or put food on the table, pay for a prostitute, or buy

> *Learn to distinguish between your needs and your wants.*

your wife a bottle of perfume. Money simply makes you more of what you already were before you had it. If you were a giver before you had money, you will still be generous once you have wealth. If your focus was always the acquisition of riches, money will just feed your desire for more. Money shows your values and preferences. If I want to know who you really are, all I need to do is look at your spending habits. What you do with your money shows me what you love and value.

But the most important thing to take from Timothy's words is that it is not money that is the root of all evil; it is the *love of money* that is evil. Don't let your money be your mistress. Finance is fickle. You could be riding high one day, and the next the winds of fortune will blow you off your mountain of money into a pit of poverty. Money cannot give you love. Money cannot give you strength. Don't look to money for what only God can give you.

The "love of money" passage does not apply just to those who have, but also to those without. You can be dirt poor and have a greater heart of greed than a multimillionaire. Also, you can be so focused on your perceived godly state of poverty that, in a way, the love of money as the root of all evil applies to the pride you take in your state of lack.

Balance and Faith

Neither extreme historic view of wealth is reflective of the scriptures or the heart of God for his people. The apostle Paul eloquently put the role of wealth in its proper place when he wrote, "Not that I speak in respect of want: for I have learned, in whatsoever state I am, therewith to be content. I know both how to be abased, and I know how to abound: everywhere and in all things I am instructed both to be full and to be hungry, both to abound and to suffer need. I can do all things through Christ which strengtheneth me" (Philippians 4:11–13 KJV). He says he was contented in both states. That doesn't mean that he lacked ambition, for he was both a preacher and a businessman. But it does mean that he was not controlled by his drives. He was motivated by his purpose. Paul knew how to do all things through Christ whether he had stuff or not, whether he had food on the table or not. Regardless of his financial state, he learned to draw contentment from Christ. Paul idolizes neither lack nor abundance, he simply puts them in their proper perspective. The focus is not on the amount in the checking account, but on the amount of contentment and strength drawn from the Christ in the heart.

Our brother the monk and our brother the prosperity

preacher have failed to understand the essence of Christianity. The Christian experience is one that transcends the issues of abundance or lack, and provides a contentment and peace that carries the believer through the vicissitudes of life's bull and bear markets, full and empty pantries, and abounding or overdrawn checking accounts. "I can do all things through Christ" means that he is my focus of existence. He is my source of contentment and the One who, through want and abundance, meets my needs. I trust Him. He supplies my wants and releases my prosperity in the increments I can handle. It is not because I am such a good sheep. It is that He is the good shepherd that I shall not want!

Pray this prayer with me:

Lord, heal me from the stress and the pressure that I get from worrying about my perception among my peers. Give me the gift of being satisfied by what you want me to have and when you know I can handle it. I thank you that you are teaching me to walk beside you and not in front of you. I repent for the times I got ahead of you. I regret the times you were trying to bless me and I was somewhere behind you, groveling with old issues. From this day forward I walk with you in peace and prosperity, knowing who I am, where I am, and whose I am. I am prepared to be blessed financially with the practical steps I am learning. But my focus is on you, for now I know that you are the greatest richness attainable and when I seek you first other things will happen as I prepare myself for what you have for me. Thank you for maturity coming to me spiritually, financially, and emotionally. My family will be blessed by what you are teaching me now. Amen.

3.

The Power to
Get Wealth

But thou shalt remember the LORD thy God: for it is he that giveth thee power to get wealth, that he may establish his covenant which he sware unto thy fathers, as it is this day.

DEUTERONOMY 8:18 (KJV)

God was faithful to His people Israel. After four hundred years of bondage as Egyptian slaves, they were delivered and given the deed to a well-watered land of their own. In Egypt they had nothing they could call their own. What little they received came from the momentary generosity of their earthly master's hand. They had no power or ability to improve their lot in life. Slavery had broken their will and bruised their pride. As a people, their hands of initiative were tied and feet of self-progress were shackled.

God had to wean the children of Israel from reliance on others, so He led them out of Egypt into the wilderness. I believe that one of the most damaging traits that subverts and impedes the progress of any people is dependency on others. To be reliant on someone else's kindness is an extremely vulnerable experience. He therefore had to wean them from the breast milk of dependency to the strong nutrition of self-reliance, and greater still God reliance. Pharaoh's food was ended. God often has to stop one source to open another. But please know that the ending of one source doesn't mean that the provision is finished. It just means that God has finished using that method.

> Discipline in finances is one of the signs of being a disciple.

The Master's methods may fluctuate, but his ultimate purpose remains the same. God had promised Abraham that He was going to bless his seed, and He did. When God makes a promise, He keeps His word. However, it is often required that we lay hold on the promise by acting on it in an aggressive way. We must go after it with total abandonment and commitment, and know that God's blessings don't necessarily come through the kindness of others. In fact, it is often in spite of a lack of others' kindness that God is able to perform the most mighty deeds. The miracle begins when we remove the training wheels of dependency on others.

The people of Israel whined for the familiar. Whenever God begins to wean us from the familiar we often whine, not realizing that the way to the wealth is to stand though the weaning process. The leeks and onions of Egypt were all gone, and now they had to learn to develop an appetite for *manna*. They had gone from eating out of Pharaoh's hand to believing God for their sustenance. The path of drought and famine often precedes the land of miracles. Nevertheless, God does provide spectacu-larly. God supernaturally provided strength for the journey that He ordained for them to make. Prosperity begins with strength for the journey. It goes far beyond surviving to thriving. But it starts with strength for the day.

Making the Journey

There are stages of success. No one achieves success without going through these stages. The hope I have for my generation is that we might go through them armed with the experiences of those who went before us. These stages are illustrated in the Scripture. When the people of Israel were living in Egypt, they were depending on Pharaoh. He gave them not enough. When-ever we depend on the mercies of others, it will never be enough. God delivered them from this scarcity. He led them out of Egypt, through the Red Sea, and through the wilderness, and for forty years they depended on God. He provided water from the rock when there was none, and fed them with manna. God provides just enough. The Bible says as thy days are so shall thy strength be.

He gave them just enough bread for the day, no leftovers. God will always take care of you. He will give you all that you need. But the preferred state is a collabo-rative effort with God. This is what is illustrated when the Lord delivered the Israelites out of the wilderness.

If you cannot handle the temptation to overextend your credit, get rid of all your credit cards.

He delivered them to the wilder-ness and delivered them from not

enough. God led the Israelites out of Egypt where they were slaves and had no power. This is a stage many of us have experienced. We have witnessed God's ability to sustain us in spite of the fact that we don't have enough to eat or even a place to live. God miraculously sustains us, then delivers us from this place of want. It is crucial that you not allow your progress to become paralyzed by a lack of faith brought on by a lack of funds. Don't give up and think you should stop believing in God and yourself. Don't assume that where you are is where you will always be. As He delivered the Israelites out of Egypt, He will deliver you out of your current situation of want.

He delivered them through the wilderness and delivered them to just enough. *Just enough*—I know that is not a popular condition. We don't want to be just getting by. We don't want to struggle and eke out our existence. But the reality is that God's strength and purpose is often revealed through our struggles. We tend to savor and appreciate what we earn with our sweat and tears, and learn what it is we really want and are willing to work for. Yes, "just enough" is a stage we need to go through to determine if we have the will and tenacity to go on to the final stage of success and rest comfortably in the stage of "more than enough."

> *Pay your bills on time.*

He delivered them from the wilderness and delivered them to more than enough. In Deuteronomy 8 we see a prophetic vision of a delivered, prosperous Israel. The vision was for the time after leaving the arid, barren regions of the wilderness. Their new home would be a good land: "a land of brooks of water, of fountains and depths that spring out of valleys and hills;

A land of wheat, and barley, and vines, and fig trees, and pomegranates; a land of oil olive, and honey; A land wherein thou shalt eat bread without scarceness, thou shalt not lack any thing in it" (Deuteronomy 8:7–9, KJV). Israel would move from dryness to fertility, from want to abundance, from meals of boiled, broiled, and baked manna to a virtual culinary feast for the eyes and taste buds. God delivered them from "just enough" to a land of plenty. This is where God wants us to be as well. He gives us the power to have "more than enough." But your seed of greatness will not grow without you using your faith to stretch yourself beyond your past limitations. When you work together with God and put into action the gifts he gives you, you too will be brought to a place of abundance. God wants you to have more than enough. He wants you to be financially independent. He wants you to use your faith to unlock your finances.

But Deuteronomy 8 does not just give a prophetic insight into Israel's history of deliverance and blessing for the sake of repeating the often-told story one more time. No, there is a warning within the story:

> Beware that thou forget not the LORD thy God, in not keeping his commandments, and his judgments, and his statutes, which I command thee this day: Lest when thou hast eaten and art full, and hast built goodly houses, and dwelt therein; And when thy herds and thy flocks multiply, and thy silver and thy gold is multiplied, and all that thou hast is multiplied; Then thine heart be lifted up, and thou forget the LORD thy God, which brought thee forth out of the land of Egypt, from the house of bondage . . .
>
> DEUTERONOMY 8:11–14 (KJV)

And like the people of Israel, you cannot forget the Lord. When you're in a place of plenty, when times are prosperous, you must say in your heart, "My power and the might of mine hand hath gotten me this wealth" (Deuteronomy 8:17, KJV).

Paying the minimum amount on a bill should be the exception rather than the rule.

There is a common affliction I call financial amnesia. Most people remember God when they are in a crisis. They are praying because they are in trouble, but as soon as the trouble recedes, they forget their prayers. They don't count their blessings, because they are too busy counting their money. They become blinded by their good fortune and forget the One who is the source of all that is good. They think they no longer need God because everything is going their way. They foolishly believe that all their success is due entirely to their own abilities, power, or business acumen. But they forget where those gifts come from.

The issue is: Can God trust you with success? Can you stand to worship Him for the things He has done? Many cannot. Most become so engrossed in the gifts He gives that they forget to honor the giver of the gift. Often we become so focused on the goal that we lose sight of the grace that enabled us to get the goal we were seeking.

The temptation for Israel is the same for those of us who came up in poverty. We can very easily get caught up in the success and once-unimaginable prosperity. When we had nothing, we praised God with abandonment. Now that we have a little something we are more dignified and austere. Our testimony was once "Look what the Lord has done," but when He really gets around to doing something significant, we become politically correct and keep the name of Jesus locked behind our lips when questioned about our success.

The danger for any impoverished people who enter their Promised Land is the danger of forgetting where we came from. A little food in the stomach will make yesterday's hunger seem years in the past. Some nice clothes in the closet and a new sofa in the living room will make the well-worn, outdated frocks and threadbare sofa you once owned seem like ancient history. Israel was continually admonished to remember where they came from lest in their prosperity they forget the Lord. For Israel and for us, the admonition is clear: Never forget that it is God who gives us the power to get the wealth.

You Got the Power

When I was a little boy, I was driven by an ambitious need to succeed. While other children played ball and tag, I was steeped in a desire to create my future and fulfill my dreams. My mother and I grew vegetables in our garden. It was a hobby, but it was hard work. I sold the vegetables we didn't eat for extra money. Little Tommy Jakes walking down the street carrying bags of vegetables was a common sight in my neighborhood. During the harvest season, I was out every day, dragging those heavy bags up and down the hills of West Virginia like an old peddler. The weight of the bags of greens bowed my back and caused my feet

> *Every month, send in fifty dollars more than your mortgage payment.*

to ache. To the average person there was just collards or kale greens, mustards or turnips greens crammed into a bag. But to the discerning eye there was far more than greens crammed in the bag. There were the secret principles of greatness in the bag. There was the lesson of going after what you wanted, the courage of knocking on a door, dealing with rejection sometimes, rudeness other times, but still pressing toward your goal with a relentlessness that was stronger than a few insults could eradicate. And although those bags of vegetables were heavy, I persevered. All dreams are heaviest in infancy. If all that you carry is easy to handle, you will never develop your potential.

Yes, I was raised carrying bags of greens. I was raised to carry my weight. Like an ant carrying a morsel of bread to his dwelling place, greatness is often dragged by persons who seem too small to carry what they believe but are far too stubborn to leave it behind. With bags of greens I learned to be tenacious and relentless, to carry my destiny even when I thought it was too heavy, and to persevere through the pain. Today when I tell young men who have difficulty finding a job to create one, I do so because I learned as a little boy that if success doesn't come after you, you have to go after it.

Buy your checks from someplace other than your bank. It will save you money.

I went from selling greens to selling shoes. I got a paper route and I arose early every morning to make deliveries. An industrious spirit has no time to wait on glamour. It didn't matter what I was working with; it only mattered where I was going and how relentlessly I pursued my dreams. Before long I noticed that God had blessed me. I didn't think about the blessings at the time, but I later realized that Psalms 1:3 (KJV) was right when it said, "Whatsoever he doeth shall prosper." God blesses what you do, not what you think, dream, or fantasize. He blesses what you do. In each of us lies a seed of greatness, a potential, and a gift. My gift was in my tenacity and entrepreneurial spirit. My gift was in the dreams that stayed in my soul. Even when my eyes were awake, I still dreamed. I was a daydreamer, a water-walker, and a bridge-builder. If you can trace down your gift and identify your dream, you have the power to get up and move on. Achievers start now. Get on your mark, get set, and go! You cannot wait on opportunity. The opportunity is the breath in your body and the strength of your mind. If you use your gifts wisely, there is no telling what you can do. But God only blesses what you do. We must be doers. We must be people of action. It all boils down to your faith in the fact that you have the power to change what is hindering you.

Deuteronomy 8:18 says that God gives us not wealth, but the power to get wealth. There is a big difference between the two. If I outright give you a twenty-dollar bill, there is little you can do but receive it. On the other hand, if I place a twenty-dollar bill on a high shelf and give you the authority to go and get it, you must stand up, walk to the shelf, and find a ruler or stick to reach up and knock the bill off the shelf, thus obtaining the reward. Too many believers are sitting around on overstuffed sofas waiting for God to drop wealth into their lap. Unfortunately, most will still be sitting there next year and the following year, with empty laps. A dream without a corresponding action aggravates the soul and leads to nothing. Put your dreams in your actions. Your actions will determine whether you are just a dreamer or an achiever.

God will give you the power to get wealth, but you will have to take the power and get a plan and work the plan to make it happen. The Hebrew word translated as "power" is *koach,* meaning literally a good or bad force, or figuratively the capacity or means. God gives us the capacity or means to get wealth. That power is in your will. It is in your talents. It is in your creativity.

The Thoughts That Change the World

In the beginning was the Word, and the Word was with God, and the Word was God. He was with God in the beginning. Through him all things were made; without him nothing was made that has been made. In him was life, and that life was the light of men.

JOHN 1:1–4 (NIV)

The term used in John, Chapter 1, translated as "word" is *logos.* It literally means the expression of a thought. Verse 3 declares that all things that are tangible were made from the expression of a thought. The world was created by a thought that God had. The thought became a word and the word became matter. If that is hard for you to conceive, consider that all buildings begin as thoughts and are then drawn into architectural plans. These sketches are physical manifestations of abstract ideas. Never laugh at someone who has an idea. Ideas are the ingredients of change. Almost everything you have in your home, from your closets to the clothes in them, are the result of someone's thoughts. From Broadway to NASA, all that we see around us are thoughts turned into physical reality.

Have you ever stopped to realize that most money is made as the result of a good idea? Some of the wealthiest people in the world got where they are because they had an idea for a better way to cook chicken, or a way to write a computer program. What is your idea? What are you thinking? Whatever you are thinking, that

> *Do your banking with a credit union rather than a bank, where fees are usually higher.*

is what you are creating in your life. When God gives you the power to get wealth, one of those powers so often ignored is a divine thought. If you have a brain, you can think and can come up with good ideas. No one has, or ever will, corner the market on good ideas. We all have the capacity to come up with ground-breaking ideas. As Christians we have the added advantage of the Holy Spirit living within us. Yes, the Holy Spirit does inspire for the preaching of the Word and the flowing of the gifts of the Spirit. But why can't the Spirit of the Living God, the Creator who made everything that has been made and knows everything about everything in creation, give you the gift to come up with business ideas? Many of us are full of Holy Spirit–inspired creative ideas that have never been worked out into reality because we have failed to make and carry out a plan. These are the seeds of greatness many let rot on the ground of excuses. Of course there are challenges and obstacles, but there are also rewards. God spoke what He thought and it became what He said. What are you talking about? And more important, what are you reaching toward?

We all have talents. They are gifts from God, the manifestation of the Holy Spirit within us. My gift may be different from yours, but they have the same source. Years ago, God dropped an idea for a women's Bible class in my heart. That idea grew and became a book, a conference, a play, and a music CD. God gave me the ability to take that idea and package it to reach a much larger audience than it would have reached if it had remained just a Bible class. As a businessman, I am successful because I see and understand the capacity God has given me and am maximizing my moment.

I am very blessed. I have my ministry, which is my passion, and I have business success, which is the result of my creativity and the source of my financial success. For years I have worked beyond my church with businesses and companies, exploring creativity without forsaking my calling to the ministry. My success comes from my working with the power that God has given me to generate wealth through the marketing of ideas. Creativity is the source of wealth, and creativity comes from the Creator. Is my success based on who I am and what I can do? Yes and no. I know and acknowledge that it is the Lord who gives all of us the power. But what will we do with that power He gives us? I equally understand that I must take what He's put within and work it out. Now I want to be the coach who motivates you to action and helps you excavate the creativity God has empowered you with. I want to shine a light on the untapped potentials that are lying dormant inside you. That creative idea He breathed into you will work if you work it.

Sowing into Good Soil

The gift, talent, or ability God gave you is your key to success. God did not give it to you to be put on display behind a glass showcase. He did not give it to you to waste. Nor did He give it to you for you to hide and deny it out of a false sense of religious humility. God gave you a gift to be poured out, used, and invested.

The term *talent* means, literally, a weight of coins or money. The talents in Matthew 25 were given, five, two, and one, to each man according to his ability. God gives you what you can handle—no more, no less. You may not have as much as your neighbor, but how much you have is not the issue; it is what you do with what you have. The man who received five traded them until he obtained five more. The man who received two also traded until he received an additional two. The original benefactor commended both men when he returned from his journey. They were lauded as good and faithful servants, and their faithfulness over little reaped them the reward of being made rulers over much.

The gentleman who received the one talent did not do as his brethren. Motivated by fear, he took the one talent and buried it in the ground. When the benefactor heard this news, he replied, "Thou wicked and slothful servant, thou knewest that I reap where I sowed not, and gather where I have not strawed: Thou oughtest therefore to have put my money to the exchangers, and then at my coming I should have received mine own with usury. Take therefore the talent from him, and give it unto him which hath ten talents. For unto every one that hath shall be given, and he shall have abundance: but from him that hath not shall be taken away even that which he hath. And cast ye the unprofitable servant into outer darkness: there shall be weeping and gnashing of teeth" (Matthew 25:26–30, KJV).

Many of God's people have buried their talent out of fear and received little or no increase. Fear is one of the greatest enemies of faith. It numbs the spirit and incarcerates creativity. Get rid of your fear immediately. Part of being a good steward is doing the most with the amount God gave you. How much have you done? Are you burying what He left you like the unprofitable servant? One of the worst things you can be is an unprofitable servant. Yet most Christians do not invest a dime. The benefactor in Matthew 25 rebuked the man with one talent for not being an investor. He saved what he had, but failed to invest what he had been given. If you believe that God is really going to bless you, what are you doing about it? Invest in what you believe. Everything in life is an investment. The farmer invests seeds for a harvest. Marriage is an investment. You can't expect a harvest where there has been no investment.

Many people are struggling because they have not used what God has given them. God gives you an acorn; you invest it and it will become a tree! Stop praying for trees while acorns are lying all over the ground. God answered your prayer for the tree when he sent you the acorn. Your creative ideas are acorns from which mighty trees emerge. Your talent is given you to be multiplied.

God gives you the power, but if you bury it out of fear you will not only miss out on multiplied talents, but you also risk the loss of that which you have been given. Have you noticed that generous people usually have a steady flow of resources in their lives? As they pour out, investing in the lives of others, they are constantly filled up. Those who are stingy and fearful of losing what they have, and hide it away, will in the end actually lose what they have. If God has given you a talent, use it or you lose it.

Financial success will come only to those who take what they have been given and invest it, plant it in good soil in hopes of a good harvest. What do I mean by this? I mean you should invest your money in profitable companies, invest your time in worth-while projects. I mean you should plant your seed of an idea in fertile ground, making sure the timing, resources, and people involved all support the idea and help it grow. The richer the soil, the more the nutrients, the better chances for a good harvest. A small grain of wheat can grow into a healthy stalk of wheat whose heavy-laden head can carry multiplied grains of wheat. Your small seedlike idea, when planted in the right soil and enriched by power from the Lord, can bring you a great harvest.

Why does the Lord Himself give you the power to get wealth? Ultimately, it is not just that you would be comfortable and financially established. God is not offended by opulence or He would never have created Heaven with gold streets. God doesn't mind you having money, but he minds money having you. Prosperity is part of the process, but it is not the objective. The objective is to become a conduit whereby currency flows through you like electricity through metal. Money is called currency because it is meant to flow like the currents of a river. As it flows, some of it will moisten the parched ground of your personal life. Some will flow through to your children and your family. And some will flow through you to bless the ministry that is helping you become all you can be. I am shocked at how little currency flows through and to Christians. Jesus said, "My people are destroyed for the lack of knowledge" (Hosea 4:6 NKJV). As you gain the knowledge, God will give you the power to gain.

Remember that God gives the power to get wealth. So we want to worship not the gift, but the Giver of the gift. The more He blesses you, the more you ought to bless Him and let the currency flow. If you do not, you will tragically make the mistake of cleaving to the gift and leaving the Giver. God is greater than any resource He chooses to give you.

How can you guard against money becoming a god in your life? It begins with an understanding—understanding that money is a tool. It can be used for evil or it can be used for good. The reason God wants godly people to have it is so that it might flow back to the ministry. Listen to the Scripture as it says, "that he may establish his covenant which he sware unto thy fathers, as it is this day" (Deuteronomy 8:18, KJV). His covenant is established when we use his provision and power to get wealth to bring glory to His name and establish His Kingdom among the nations. Supporting God's work is why He gives us the power to get wealth. But we must also understand that sowing into a ministry is only part of the plan. Investing, saving, thinking thoughts that are prosperous and progressive—these are also a prerequisite for the next move of God. Are you working for your money or is your money working for you? Get your money out of the ground, you unprofitable servant, and put your money to work!

Father, I pray for those reading that You would grant unto them the wisdom needed to determine what is good ground. I pray that they might become tithers and givers. I also pray that they might become investors and thinkers. Stir them up so that they are both practical and powerful, obeying the Word and yet wise in the ways of the world's systems. Give them today the power to get wealth, and when they have it give them the humility to honor you with their increase. In Jesus' name, amen.

4.

The Power of Compounding

Nature paints us a vivid picture of the power of compounding. Most of us have never lived on a farm, so we know little about agrarian principles, but every farmer knows that a little seed, planted in good soil and well tended, will produce a harvest exponentially greater than the original seed. For example, each seed of corn invested in the ground has the potential to grow into a stalk that will minimally produce a couple ears of corn, each ear containing numerous kernels. Likewise, when the investor plants his money in stocks, bonds, mutual finds, or any of a number of investment options, he will receive a return that is greater than his initial investment. A seed of money planted at a certain interest rate will grow exponentially over the years if it remains untouched. For example, $2,000 invested in the stock market at 11 percent interest per year would be worth about $53,416.19 after 30 years. Compounded interest causes money to grow greater the longer it is planted. Two dollars a day invested at a 13.17 percent annual return (the annual stock market return since 1950) will grow to over $1 million after 46 years. So if you start early in life and invest a minimal amount (two dollars per day is the price of a loaded hamburger), you can potentially retire as a millionaire. But like the farmer, you have to plant something to get a harvest.

Another farming principle that we would be wise to emulate in our financial dealings is saving some seed from the harvest for future plantings. The farmer cannot con-sume or sell his entire harvest; he must keep a bit to put back in the ground so that he can have a fruitful crop next year. Similarly, when we have the good fortune to come into some money, we should take a portion and reinvest so that we will have income in the days to come. If you have a take-home pay of $20,000 per year and spend it all on eating out at the finest restaurants and purchasing the latest fashion designer clothes, you will have a full stomach and a packed closet, but your pockets will be empty. If instead you invested even 10 percent—$2,000 per year—in, say, a mutual fund that averaged a 15 percent return per year, after ten years you would have over $49,000. After twenty years that amount grows to just about $267,000. And in thirty years you could retire as a millionaire with more than $1,200,000. Are you willing to give up a few dinners out and a couple of pairs of new shoes to be a millionaire? The choice is yours.

Now, when I say invest, I don't mean "investing" in the

> *Don't waste your hard-earned money on the lottery or games of chance; invest it instead.*

weekly lottery. Unfortunately, too many of our generation have developed a lottery mentality. People think that if they could just get lucky and pick the winning numbers, they can have an instant fortune and live comfortably for the rest of their lives. The truth is you have a better chance of being struck by lightning. The odds are stacked against you. Yet the sad fact is that people spend millions and millions of dollars each year in these get-rich-quick lotteries that leave them with high hopes and low bank accounts. What's sadder still is that of the few who do win, many are broke within a year. They hit the jackpot and spend it all on new cars, fur coats, and diamond rings. They take their newfound wealth and throw it away on luxury items. Now, I'm not saying that if you have the means you shouldn't enjoy the finer things in life, but it is plain foolish to spend all of your money on a fancy sports car and then not be able to afford the gas to put in it. Much smarter is the winner who takes his prize and invests it wisely, for then he can enjoy the continued returns.

Whenever money comes into your hands, make sure a portion is reinvested. If you faithfully keep some seed for future planning, like the smart farmer, you will never go hungry.

Debt Without Honor

The main reason people get into financial trouble is that they allow themselves to get caught in the debt trap. So many people don't know how to handle delayed gratification. We are so bombarded with the new, the flashy, and the up-to-date,

> *You are more likely to get hit by lightning than win the lottery.*

and we buy into the message that we must have the latest fad or fashion *now.* We have forgotten how to scrimp and save. Why should we wait and save for something when our line of credit allows us to make the purchase, have it delivered to our doorstep, and unwrap it before dinner is served? We do not understand how to live within our present financial means. We run up credit-card debt for things that we can't afford so that we will be able to keep up with the Jones family. The burden of debt has become so great for so many that filing for bankruptcy has become an acceptable and commonplace financial escape hatch instead of an option that once was considered late in the game only after all other recourses were exhausted.

You should not run up credit-debt for things that are neither necessary for your daily living nor within your financial means to afford. Your lifestyle needs to be determined by your present income, not what you wish it would be. You shouldn't be buying all that jewelry from that home shopping show when you're unable to pay your bills and the electric company is threatening to shut off the power. How dare you wear designer clothes when your children's teeth are rotting because you can't afford to send them to the dentist? Forget the Jones family, Smith family, or any other family up or down the block; don't try to keep up with anyone. Live within your means.

Credit cards carry high-interest rates. Large debt at a high-interest rate is the antithesis of the compounding principle. Instead of you getting the payback from the planted seed, over time you pay the equivalent of a few ears of corn to borrow a couple seeds. High-interest debt is essentially economic slavery.

When you owe another, your freedom is impaired. Your ability to decide your destiny is tainted by the amount you owe. Your labors will extend for years, paying off something you bought many moons ago, that is now torn and worn and sits forgotten in a corner of the basement or garage.

> *Render therefore to all their dues: tribute to whom tribute is due; custom to whom custom; fear to whom fear; honour to whom honour. Owe no man any thing, but to love one another: for he that loveth another hath fulfilled the law.*
>
> ROMANS 13:7–8 (KJV)

Except for major purchases (a home, real estate, business ventures, school loans, or an automobile whose monthly payments you can afford), you should use credit only to live within your means: to purchase items you have budgeted for and can pay off quickly.

Determine your lifestyle and stick to it. An increase in income does not necessarily mean that you need to increase your consumption. If you get some extra seed, you need to seriously consider eat-

Seedtime and harvest are biblical principles that work.

ing only what you need, and planting the rest back in investments and savings. A recent best-selling book titled *The Millionaire Next Door* revealed that most millionaires in the United States do not have extravagant lifestyles. They live comfortably, but at a level well below what they can afford. Many buy their suits off the rack, purchase only used cars, and clip coupons from the paper.

Are they being overly frugal? No, their priority has been to not eat all their seed, but to put it back in investments that produce a greater harvest over the long haul.

You must determine what your lifestyle priorities are and live accordingly. Your decisions must be based on your plan and not the pressures from family or society to live a certain way. I remember years ago when my wife and I received a financial blessing from the sales of my first book. We moved up and into a wonderful, spacious new house. The car I had at the time, which sat parked in the driveway, was somewhat dated and didn't quite match the glamour of the new house. Some of my associates suggested that I needed to get a new car to match the new house. But what they didn't understand was that I was working something for the future. I took some proceeds from the book sales and invested it in another business venture. In time, that business produced a profit and some of *that* money went to buy a new car. Yes, I eventually enjoyed the fruits of my labor, but my first concern was replanting some of the seed so that there would be fruit in the years to come.

Each According to His Means

As believers, we must allow each other the freedom to responsibly determine our own lifestyle. There have been too many years of preaching that either condemned wealth or poverty. Too many churches have attempted to set up a socioeconomic litmus test to enter the kingdom, that only the folks who live, dress, eat, and have an income according to their interpreted "biblical" standard will be acceptable. We need to dispense with judgment. Don't judge your neighbors on either their wealth or poverty. The amount of money in the bank account is not the issue; the issue is one of the heart, of their attitude before God.

Generosity is a virtue whether it comes out of a poor man or a rich man. If I have a full bank account, I have more to be accountable and responsible for than the poor man does, but the same rules apply. Equal sacrifice but unequal gifts is an often-used phrase in the church. The principle is that you may have more or less seed than the next person, but you are still called to equal generosity and sacrifice.

There is a story in the Bible about a widow woman who gave her last couple of coins in the offering plate. Jesus praised her because of her great sacrifice. Sure, others of greater means had placed significantly larger amounts in the offering, but this woman gave her all. The point of the story is that this woman had the right attitude in her heart. You may not have as much to give as your neighbor, but at your level, and with your two coins, you can still make a sacrifice.

> *Plan to save or invest a set percentage of each paycheck.*

As I have traveled around the world, I am always impressed by families and churches of humble means who go to great lengths to show hospitality to visitors. Although they cannot spread a feast like one in the home of a millionaire, they empty the pantry, pull out Grandma's special dishes, and leave you feeling like royalty.

The principle of unequal gifts but equal sacrifice can be applied to investing. You must guard against the lie that you have nothing to invest. When it comes to your future, any little bit helps. You may have to sacrifice a little something today to have a lot more in the future. The rich man up the street might have larger amounts to invest, and more income remaining after investing, yet he still makes the basic decision to delay gratification today so that he will reap more rewards tomorrow. The amount you can invest may be small, but your rewards will be great. Replant some seed and your means will continue to grow.

Work a Budget

The only way you can take control of your spending and determine your lifestyle priorities is with a budget. Unfortunately, "budget" has become a dirty word in some circles. The purpose of a budget is not to restrict your spending but to be a tool for you to determine where your money is presently going, so you can shift funds around to match your long-term goals and priorities. Our spending habits reveal our priorities more than any other area of our life. We can speak about our supposed priorities, but where our money goes is the true reflection of our priorities. As a nation we spend an enormous amount of money on cosmetics, soft drinks, cigarettes, and other nonessentials. Did you know that in 1999 Americans spent more than $18.5 billion on coffee and bought 23 billion packs of cigarettes?

Have your pay sent through your employer's direct deposit system right to your savings account.

Where is your money going? Write your expenditures down

and add them up. You might be surprised to see a large amount of money is wasted on items you could easily do without. A few dollars here and there become significant over time. Three dollars a day for a fancy latte coffee might seem like a harmless indulgence, but that's over twenty dollars a week, almost eighty-five dollars a month, and more than a thousand dollars a year that you could be investing. Put that twenty dollars a week in a mutual fund and by the time you retire you'll have a nice little nest egg.

Begin a budget by saving receipts for all spending. Each month record your expenditures in a notebook. List expenses under categories such as housing, food, utilities, and medical. After a couple of months, you'll know exactly where your money is going. Be prepared for some shocking revelations. If you have never had control over your spending, and always seem to come up short in cash before the end of the month, you will create the opportunity to not only see why you fall short but be able to take corrective measures to redirect your cash flow.

The top priority in a budget should be paying God. God should get the tithe. Tithe is a biblical term that means a tenth. This is a tenth of your gross income. If Uncle Sam gets his cut off the gross, God deserves the same. The tithe is to be given to your home church. The tithe is used to support the ministry of the church. It is a small percentage of all that God has given you, and is symbolic of the whole belonging to God. God promises that blessings will follow those who tithe. "Bring ye all the tithes into the storehouse, that there may be meat in mine house, and prove me now herewith, saith the LORD of hosts, if I will not open you the windows of heaven, and pour you out a blessing, that there shall not be room enough to receive it" (Malachi 3:10,

KJV). God can release financial increase to those who will not be controlled by the love of money. The money is not the evil; it is placing money as a god in one's life that is evil. Skimming the tithe off the top of one's income keeps the proper perspective on who owns all that we have.

> *Take full advantage of your employer's 401(k) plan.*

You must give the tithe willingly and happily. "But this I say, He which soweth sparingly shall reap also sparingly; and he which soweth bountifully shall reap also bountifully. Every man according as he purposeth in his heart, so let him give; not grudgingly, or of necessity: for God loveth a cheerful giver" (2 Corinthians 9:6–7, KJV). God does not want gifts that come from compulsion or fear. He doesn't want you to have the attitude that you are cutting a deal with Him or paying off the church. God wants gifts given out of a heart of gratitude, obedience, and trust. A generous heart will not flinch at the idea of tithing, and will always find that it gives way beyond the ten percent.

Second after paying God is paying you. Budget so that you are able to save a certain percentage of your income each month before you pay any of the other bills you owe. Determine your long-term goals: college for your children; a business venture; a comfortable retirement. Then calculate what you will need to save or invest each month to attain those goals. Set that money aside at the beginning of the month. If you do not make it a priority and spend the money on other things first, chances are you will never have enough money to achieve your goals. It is here that your budget can help. If it is a priority to save or invest a certain amount, you may find that you need to curtail spending in another area of your life to be able to have the funds to put aside. This is the same as the farmer not eating all his seed. To get a harvest a few years down the line, you must put some seed back now.

After paying God and yourself, meet all of the other financial obligations that your life entails. Start out with those that are regular bills related to housing, utilities, and other loans. These are bills that you are legally obligated to pay, and if you fail to pay on time, risk high fees or interest payments. Pay these off first. And get away from the mentality that all you need to pay is the required minimum. You need to develop the habit and money-management skills to be able to pay your bills in full when due. Otherwise you will get into a no-win cycle. Every time you don't pay a bill in full, you accrue interest on the balance. In months to come, you will find yourself writing checks to pay off the interest but the primary amount you owe will never decrease. Put as much as you can toward outstanding debt. You might have to stretch a bit, or do without for a few months, but in the end you will profit.

God Will Bless You

Let me reiterate: Plant something to get a harvest, and save some of your seed for future planting. Whatever your current financial condition, you should begin to practice these principles. Even if you are presently in a situation where you do not have much, you should implement this advice, for you will carry these habits with you if fortune should come your way. I know you think that if you get the money you will know how to handle it, but that is not necessarily so. Sudden wealth dropped on undisciplined lives will result in money that disappears quickly and stresses that can lead to broken homes and marriages. Why should God bless you with prosperity if it will destroy you?

Fortune attained quickly lacks the process that produces real wisdom. The greatest part about receiving the blessings is the process that you went through to gain it. The endurance, perseverance, and hard work necessary for success prepare you to plant and receive multiple harvests. It is your wisdom and ability to handle success that causes God to invest in you even more. You have to attain the ability to be a good steward over every opportunity in order to have the good success that God has promised his people. God is a businessman. He is not going to do business with someone who shows no sign of potential return. He invests in people who demonstrate an ability to handle what He has given them.

God gave Adam and Eve specific instructions. He told them to be fruitful, multiply, replenish, subdue, and have dominion. When we apply these directions to our finances, the message is clear. In financial matters, to be fruitful means to produce income. Multiplying would refer to investing and making your money grow. We must also replenish, or restore, the sources of our success. This could mean giving something back to our family, our community, or our church. Then there is the command to subdue, which suggests controlling the things that could potentially get out of control. Maintain control over your finances; don't let money control you. If you do all these things, you will have dominion. A dominion is a kingdom. If you abide by these four principles, God will bless you with a kingdom of good fortune.

Then he said to those standing by, "Take his mina away from him and give it to the one who has ten minas." "Sir," they said, "he already has ten!" He replied, "I tell you that to everyone who has, more will be given, but as for the one who has nothing, even what he has will be taken away."

LUKE 19:24–27 (NIV)

God says he will give more to the one who has more. It seems strange, but it is true. He knows that the one who has more has demonstrated the mastery over what he has been given. The greater domains are given to those who possess the greatest ability to manage God's blessings. If you have sound financial practices and successfully manage your money, God will invest in you. He is looking for fruitfulness, and when He finds it He will reward it with more fruit and finally with much fruit. He will compound blessings on those who have managed what he has given them with good stewardship and integrity.

"I am the true vine, and my Father is the gardener. He cuts off every branch in me that bears no fruit while every branch that does bear fruit he prunes so that it will be even more fruitful."

JOHN 15:1–2 (NIV)

"This is to my Father's glory, that you bear much fruit, showing yourselves to be my disciples."

JOHN 15:8 (NIV)

There is a compounded blessing waiting for you. You haven't seen the half of what God can do when you apply these principles and adhere to the word of God. In the words of the old hymn, "We shall go rejoicing bringing in the sheaves." God has promised compounded blessings, and He is waiting for you to gather and bring them in.

5.

A Plan to Get Wealth

And let them make me a sanctuary; that I may dwell among them. According to all that I shew thee, after the pattern of the tabernacle, and the pattern of all the instruments thereof, even so shall ye make it.

EXODUS 25:8–9 (KJV)

In Exodus 25:9, God told Moses to build a sanctuary according to a pattern, according to a plan. This phrase is one of the most important ones in all of Scripture. It is repeated over and over again to men who are progressive and life changers. It is the secret to prosperity and effectiveness. I want to share its significance with you so that you can use it to build your life and accomplish your goals. This is God's directive: Build according to a plan. This is wise counsel that many have ignored. If there is to be any lasting accomplishments, we must build according to plan. You must have a plan or you have planned inadvertently to fail. Your future is a direct derivative of the plans you place in motion today.

I can remember when I was a child there were houses that were built without blueprints. Much like the raising of an old barn, the house would be built by the neighbors who had free time and extra lumber. I am sure budgetary constraints were the primary reason for such mayhem. But the truth of the matter is that it often cost more money in the long run. The homes were so poorly built that even more money had to be spent to fix the faulty construction. You should have seen some of the bowed walls and leaking septic tanks built in those days. What a mess it was.

> *Deposit any refunds, bonuses, or unexpected gifts into your savings account or investment account.*

It wasn't that the men were not capable. Some of the men were very talented. But without a plan, their talents weren't directed toward a unified goal. The building process was haphazard and the result was a failure. A plan tailors talents and directs them toward a specific goal. All people have some talent, but without a plan they fall short of their goals. Now, I know that every plan may not be flawless and may require adjustments as you go along, but even the weakest plan forces the planner to prepare. And when you prepare you will be better able to handle the inevitable and unforeseeable bumps on the road toward your goal.

Today, every major construction project begins with blueprints. Any building begins with an idea. An architect takes that idea and creates on paper a sketch—a plan—that carpenters and skilled laborers will follow. They will build according to the plan that is drawn. No one would think of building a skyscraper without an architect. Yet many people attempt to build financial strength without a plan. You need a plan for anything of significance in your life. If you accrue wealth, you need estate planning. If you invest, you need investment planning. If you're going to have a surgery, there is consultation and surgical planning. No matter what the task, success demands an effective plan.

Now, every plan begins with a desire, a goal, or a dream. In other words, it all starts with an idea. If you have no idea, you have no hope of accomplishment. Prayer is essential, but faith without works is dead. You must have a plan for your financial well-being, and it needs to include where you are, where you want to go, and how you will maintain what you have when you get there. Let's discuss a wonderful Bible illustration of great planning.

The Dream

Joseph, the favored son of Israel, dreamed a dream. In his dream he saw a day when he would be exalted and his family would bow down before him in subjection. His brothers took great offense at Joseph's sharing of the dream and conspired to put him to death. Through the intervention of his brother Reuben, Joseph was spared death, stripped and placed in a deep pit, and eventually sold into slavery to some traders on their way to the land of Egypt. In Egypt, Potipher, an officer of Pharaoh, purchased him. God gave Joseph much favor:

> And his master saw that the LORD was with him, and that the
> LORD made all that he did to prosper in his hand. And Joseph

found grace in his sight, and he served him: and he made him
overseer over his house, and all that he had he put into his hand.
And it came to pass from the time that he had made him overseer
in his house, and over all that he had, that the LORD blessed the
Egyptian's house for Joseph's sake; and the blessing of the LORD
was upon all that he had in the house, and in the field.

GENESIS 39:3–5 (KJV)

Joseph's favored position was quickly challenged. Potipher's wife desired Joseph sexually. Joseph refused because he understood that Potipher had given him great authority and shown him great favor. During a visit to her chamber, Potipher's wife snatched Joseph's garment and accused him of attempting to rape her. Joseph ended up thrown in prison. In prison Joseph's favor continued and he was given charge over all the prisoners in the place (Genesis 39:21–23). It was in prison that Joseph became known for interpreting dreams, a gift that eventually came to the ears of Pharaoh himself, who called Joseph out of prison to interpret two disturbing dreams revealing a future prolonged famine. Joseph not only interpreted the dreams but gave Pharaoh a plan for how to work the national food supply to prepare for the years of famine that were to come. When it came time to hire the man for the job, Pharaoh turned to Joseph and said, "Joseph, Forasmuch as God hath shewed thee all this, there is none so discreet and wise as thou art: Thou shalt be over my house, and according unto thy word shall all my people be ruled: only in the throne will I be greater than

The giving of tithes opens the windows of heaven.

thou. And Pharaoh said unto Joseph, See, I have set thee over all the land of Egypt" (Genesis 41:39–41, KJV).

Joseph's plan directed Egypt to save up a portion of her grain supply during the years of plenty, so when famine hit she had full storehouses of grain to feed her own people and those of the surrounding nations. Eventually, during the height of the famine, Joseph's own family made the trip to Egypt to ask for food. Joseph's original dream of his exaltation became reality when his own family bowed before him in honor, requesting their next meal. Though his dream was delayed by the jealousy of those around him, it was not denied.

This story of Joseph illustrates five important concepts that are essential to achieving success in any endeavor.

1. Faith in the Favor of God

Joseph walked in the favor that was on his life. Favor will come to your life when you understand who God is and who you are, and when you find out your unique purpose in life in the light of God's will. God turned into good all the evil that man brought on Joseph. God gave him a dream, and Joseph continued to walk toward his destiny even in the pits and prisons of life. Yes, God's favor can still be present in your life even in the most unpleasant of circumstances. God's gift to Joseph was a dream that sustained him through all of his hardships. It is the dream that keeps us alive while we wait on its fulfillment. Just as a carrot placed in front of a horse causes him to gallop more swiftly, people with a dream before them run the race with tenacity because they are motivated by their goal.

Joseph was highly favored. He was raised with the kind of support that is always required for greatness. I believe that children who are well nurtured, as Joseph was, fare better than those who are left to grow without proper affirmation. I know you are thinking that it is not good to favor one child over another, but you must realize that favor didn't come from his father. It might have come *through* his father, but it came from God. And when God gives one of his children favor, it will ultimately work for the betterment of all of them as they discover the purpose for the favor and the power they have to attain success.

> *Invest $2,000 annually in an IRA account; it can be deducted from your income tax.*

That kind of divine favor starts early and is demonstrated in every gift we are given throughout our lives. That is why it is important to take advantage of and become a good steward over the things God gave you. He knows what you need and he knows when and through whom to give it in order to enhance his ultimate purpose in your life. I have always considered myself favored by God. That surely doesn't mean that I was perfect. Oh no. Nor did it mean that my life went perfectly, either. But it does mean that in spite of all obstacles, by the grace of God, I continued and progressed because I knew that the Lord was with me. You must know that for yourself. No one can make you know you are highly favored. That is something that one senses in the depths of your being, and you need that knowledge to usher you into your destiny.

2. Identify Your Gifting

God gives each of us our own unique gifts. It is our job to recognize these gifts, nurture them, and utilize them to live up to our full potential. There is something or someone in your life that is a gift from God. Open your eyes! Don't sit there with your head in your hands feeling sorry for what you don't have. Look around you and inside of you and recognize what you do have. It may be an artistic talent, a business talent, or strength of character. It may be an opportunity or a person in your life that can show you the way. God gives you the resources for success. But it is up to you to recognize them and use them to their fullest.

You may wish you had the voice of Mahalia Jackson, the athletic ability of Kobe Bryant, or the entrepreneurial skills of Donald Trump. Their gifts are certainly admirable, but they are not yours, nor are they mine. We each have our own, special, unique gifts designated just for us. No one can use another man's gift in place of his own. It is like spending money that is not in your account. If you are going to be effective, you must be prepared to spend out of the rich resources of your own unique gifting and abilities. Many people do not succeed because they have more appreciation in what God has given someone else than they do in their own resources and gifts. Many aspire to imitate greatness in others rather than to excavate the greatness that is in themselves. You must identify your own gifts and then use them.

The longer you invest in the stock market, the lower your risk.

Joseph continued to faithfully use his gifts and abilities

throughout all the stages of his life. He was gifted in administration and had great wisdom and insight from God to plan for success. He administrated affairs in the prison as faithfully as he did in Potipher's house and Pharaoh's kingdom. Your plan to get wealth must include a willingness to do what you do best regardless of whether you are in the spotlight or behind the scenes, if you receive adequate compensation or are underpaid. The path of favor in our lives leads through many economic ups and downs, through success and seeming failure, through pits, prisons, and palaces. "A man's gift maketh room for him, and bringeth him before great men" (Proverbs 18:16, KJV). If you follow your dream, and faithfully use what God has gifted you with, your gift will open the doors you need to succeed.

3. The Power of a Plan

Joseph had a plan. Many people fail to attain their financial goals because they have no plan. It is not enough to have a dream. A dream is a seed. The talent is important also, as your dream cannot exceed your talent. But talent is water poured on a seed. As the seed must have water, the dream must be dreamed by someone with the talent to do what they are dreaming of or it cannot occur. But none of that is going to give long-term success without a plan. A plan takes all your dreams and talents and maximizes them by bringing structure to the concept. A plan puts soil in a pot, plants the seed, and regulates the temperature and watering schedule so that the seed becomes a healthy plant.

We've already spoken about some of the main components of a plan for financial prosperity: setting a budget, living within your means, and planting some of your seed into savings and investments for a future harvest. A plan for financial success will involve some fundamental changes in your attitudes and actions. It will take discipline to make and keep accountable to a budget. It will take a change in your thinking to break free of the temptation to live off the plastic—by that I mean the credit cards—and to not eat all of your seed. It will take steadfast commitment to plant your money in good ground—in tithes and offerings as well as sound investments. It takes both the spiritual and the practical for you to have good success. But remember, the idea is not to get rich but to be blessed. The Bible says, "The blessings of the Lord maketh rich and addeth no sorrow to it" (Proverbs 10:22, KJV). So being blessed may bring riches, but it is not riches alone. Riches without the father's blessing add much sorrow to life, and that we do not need.

> *Don't raise your standard of living the next time you get a raise; invest it instead.*

Not only did Joseph have a plan, but he worked out the specific details to see the plan through. His plan included specific goals and amounts of grain to be saved. He conceived the plan and then worked it out. You, too, will need to stay on top of your plan and work it out. It will work if you work it. No plan is successful if it is just a theory. It must be put into action. Your plan should be written out, and it must include specific actions and deadlines to fulfill those actions.

4. Giving Is the Cycle That Releases More

The accumulation of wealth should never be the Christian's final goal. Wealth in the Kingdom is not the end, but the means to the end. The end is that the gospel will be preached to the entire world and broken lives be redeemed and restored. Ultimately, God should be our financial advisor. Just like the supply of manna given to the Israelites in the wilderness, so will be our financial supply. If we take what He gives and use it as He commands, the supply will continue. If we are generous, God will continue to be generous to us. But if, like the Israelites, we hoard our supply, we will find that in time it will dry up.

Don't get me wrong, I believe in saving. But saving is different from hoarding. When you save, you put something aside for future use. Joseph's plan incorporated saving. He directed the Egyptians to save some grain in a time of plenty so that they would have enough when famine struck. But that grain was not just to feed Egypt; it also blessed all the surrounding nations and even Joseph's family, who had stripped him, dumped him in a pit, and sold him into slavery. Generosity was part of Joseph's plan.

Generosity is a spiritual investment principle that works. Now, I'm not saying you must give away all you have and live like a pauper in order to be blessed. Everything you do must have balance. You must use what you are given, maximize these gifts, and use them to fulfill your needs so you can fulfill your duty to serve the Kingdom. But it is important that your needs do not become so overwhelming that you neglect to seek and find opportunities to give. Generosity protects us from falling prey to the sin of serving money. You are not to serve money. Money is to serve you, and you should serve God by using it according to His plan.

5. Ten Percent Is Not Yours but Belongs to God

As we discussed before, paying the tithe to the work of the Kingdom is a key to breaking the temptation to hoard what we have, and a key to releasing the blessings of God in our life. The tithe reminds us that all we have belongs to God. The tithe is ten percent of our gross income given to support the work of the local church. Our numeric system is based on groups of ten; ten is actually as high as anyone need count, as all other numbers are repetitions of the same. When we give God ten percent, we are symbolically saying that all that I have belongs to You. It is the highest honor, as it is the highest number we can reach without repetition.

It is a disgrace that many pay tithes after they have deducted for the government, social security, the credit union, and so on. What an insult to God that you honestly report your gross income to the government but deceitfully alter that gross when it comes to God. Jesus said, "Render therefore to Caesar the things that are Caesar's, and to God the things that are God's" (Matthew 22:21, NKJV). In other words, pay both God and the government what they are entitled to. Isn't God entitled to all that we have? Paying Him

Teach your children money-management skills when they are young and they will carry those lessons throughout their lives.

should be a priority above all else. Are you giving God what is right or are you giving God what is left?

When we give the tithe, we not only honor God but we let Him know that our commitment to His work is greater than our commitment to money. It lets Him know that our primary purpose is serving His kingdom and any blessings He gives us will go toward that purpose. The tithe is seed-planted into the kingdom of God, and just like investments in the stock market, it will produce a harvest. The harvest may come soon or it may come later, but God will release blessing to those who faithfully, obediently, and generously give.

Joseph was a tithe from his family. Had he not been given, they would have later starved to death in famine. Although the circumstances and motives surrounding his deportation to Egypt were cruel, he was given first from his family, and later became a harvest for his family. The sacrifice of Joseph opened the way for immeasurable blessing to his family during a time of desperate need.

Your tithe and other gifts may seem like a great sacrifice now, and the payback may not come in a form, fashion, or time frame that you presently perceive. But the blessing will catch up with you in time. You may not see a check in the mail on Monday to compensate for the money you placed in the offering plate on Sunday, but in time you will see His blessing.

The blessing may be delayed, but it will come. Take the case of the Israelites. Joseph was also a tithe from the nation of Israel. He was key to saving the Egyptian people from the seven years of famine that engulfed their nation. After Joseph was gone, the Israelites became enslaved to the Egyptians. For four hundred years the Egyptians stole the labor of the Israelites. Generations of

Israelites suffered and were not compensated for their labors. It was only the generation that left Egypt in the Exodus that received the just recompense for their work. It took four hundred years for the blessing to come.

> . . . the children of Israel did according to the word of Moses; and they borrowed of the Egyptians jewels of silver, and jewels of gold, and raiment: And the LORD gave the people favour in the sight of the Egyptians, so that they lent unto them such things as they required. And they spoiled the Egyptians.
>
> EXODUS 12:35–36 (KJV)

Israel had a right to the wealth of Egypt for two reasons: first, because it was Joseph, the tithe, a son of Israel, who strategized the survival of Egypt from famine; and second, because for four hundred years they were oppressed as slaves in the very land their forefathers had served so faithfully. There is no other way to interpret this Exodus passage than to see that God was paying Israel back for her years of uncompensated labor and for the faithfulness of her father Joseph as a tithe of blessing to the Egyptian people. Joseph faithfully served God's purpose, as did the Israelites for four hundred years, and the spoils of Egypt were the interest accrued from years of dedicated living.

We should model our lives after Joseph. He was a dreamer, he was a planner, he was a faithful servant of God. His trust in the Lord, his understanding of God's purpose for him, and his unwavering commitment to fulfill that purpose saved a nation from destruction and released a financial miracle for his family for generations to come. As it was with Joseph, so shall it be with you. God has a financial plan for your life and your family, and through it your generations will be blessed. Plan your work and work your plans, and the riches of the Kingdom will be yours now and forever.

Part Two

FAMILY

6.

Family Matters

I find it disconcerting that most of the teaching on family coming out of the Christian community deals with ideals and not reality. We present a vision of family life that comes from classic television: a working father, a stay-at-home mother, two children, a dog, four goldfish, and a two-car garage attached to a ranch home in suburbia. Young men and women are virgins when they enter into marriage and come together in holy matrimony to form a partnership based on a foundation of trust, communication, and mutual respect. With great joy, but careful consideration, they take on their roles as parents, fulfilling God's directive to be fruitful and multiply. They raise their children to be good Christians, and by example instill in them the values of hard work, strong morals, and compassion. As a unit, the family is productive, not only raising themselves up, but in doing so giving something to their community and their church. Children go to college, work hard, get good jobs, and eventually start families of their own. Proud parents, grandparents, and great-grandparents look on with satisfaction, knowing they fulfilled their duty and can rest in the comfort that they passed on a worthy legacy that will serve generations to come.

While the ideal is wonderful and an admirable goal for any family, the reality of family life as we enter the twenty-first century is far more complex. Our families represent a portrait of diversity ranging from single mothers with several children, grandparents taking care of grandbabies, and blended families. The Ozzie and Harriet scenario does not ring true for the majority of us. More often than not, family means fighting, and home is a horror of screaming mates, troubled kids, financial chaos, and general dysfunction.

> *Love is patient, love is kind. It does not envy, it does not boast, it is not proud. It is not rude, it is not self-seeking, it is not easily angered, it keeps no record of wrongs.*
> 1 CORINTHIANS 13:4–5 (NIV)

I fear that since many Americans cannot relate to the ideals the Church teaches, they come to regard those teachings as outdated and irrelevant. But the fundamental principles are timeless and well worth applying to our lives. The challenge is to find a way for grace to enter and become pertinent to the realities of your family circumstances. I would like to address the family as it exists in homes across America, and, I hope, help you maximize the potential that is in your home.

Any instance of success must have a starting point, a point of origin. A strong home base is an invaluable asset in your pursuit of any endeavor. It serves as a foundation upon which to build future accomplishments. The values and dreams instilled in you by your family form the basis of all you will achieve in this lifetime. Your family should be a support system, your lifeline in times of trouble, and a cushion if you fall. The unconditional love and acceptance will propel you to heights of greatness; the familiarity and deep understanding will anchor you and keep you steadfast on the path of right action.

You may be ready to close this book because you think your family is a mess and doesn't serve as a basis for anything but bitterness and despair. Your reality might be far from the ideal situation. You may be struggling to raise your children alone. You may have never known your father. Perhaps the last time you saw your brother was three years ago when you got into a heated argument over the money he borrowed from you and never paid back. No, your family is not the one you see on the sitcoms, where the biggest problem is a meddling but good-natured mother-in-law. Your life is more like *The Young and the Restless,* minus the stylish clothes and glamorous lifestyle. In your home there's lots of drama and no laugh track, so what can I tell you about family that will pertain to you?

First of all, I want to stress that no matter what the configuration of your household, you can have a family. One parent, grandparents, a collection of cousins living together day-to-day—it doesn't matter. Family is just a group of people working together for the good of the whole. What this means is that regardless of who comprises your family, the important thing is that you are a mutually supportive entity that shares common goals and aspirations. A family is not the individual members, but the sum total of each individual's contribution.

The second thing I want to impart to you is that although I spoke about the ideal situation, in reality there is no such thing. Every family is unique—a collective of one-of-a-kind individuals—and cannot fit in the rigid confines of five simple points in a textbook example. You see, you are a unique person, as is your mate, as is your mother, your brother, and as are your children. You each bring to the family table a complex combination of experiences, idiosyncrasies, cultural pressures, and personality styles. When you all dump your ingredients into the communal pot of family, you may find you have a sour stew of conflict. The spices clash, the sauces don't mix, and the result is a casserole full of slop not fit to feed the pigs.

My challenge to you is to start today to act like a gourmet chef. Carefully and with love, mix all your ingredients together. Stir that pot with compassion and understanding, and season the mix with support, encouragement, and respect. Don't neglect it; it might boil over or burn. Instead, tend to the pot with a watchful eye, let it simmer gently, and the flavors will blend, creating a dish fit for a king.

What's in the Pot?

There are many influences that contribute to who we are and how we relate to each other within the family. The most potent factor is our past experiences. Our experiences shape what we want and what we expect from one another. For instance, if your mother and father related only in terms of who could get in the last word or who could raise their voice the loudest, you probably have carried those dysfunctional patterns into your own marriage and have come to define love in terms of bickering and making up. If your parents' method of discipline was beatings, the bruises they inflicted were more than physical. They left you with low self-esteem, and likely you, too, raise your hands to your children. Well, it's time to break the cycle!

Your view of family relations must be cleaned up. Romans 12:2 (KJV) states, "and be not conformed to this world: but be ye transformed by the renewing of your mind, that ye may prove what is that good, and acceptable, and perfect, will of God." Your diseased and broken concepts that affect your most intimate relationships must be transformed. To do so, the first step is to be honest with yourself about your experiences and how they have shaped your views and expectations. What messages did you receive as a child that now play back when you interact as an adult? Are you letting your parents' marriage direct the path of your own relationship with your husband or wife? When you scold your children, are you reacting to your own frustration and self-hatred? Honestly assess the basis of your actions, thoughts, and perceptions. To thine own self be true.

Unique Historical Scars

Yes, we are shaped by our past experiences, but sometimes we have to go farther back into the past to find the root of our brokenness. Some of us are shaped by our history. Being five generations from slavery, I know that one of the most damaging aspects of slavery was not the beatings—though they were horrendous. It was not the murders, as reprehensible as they were. The greatest atrocity, the one that has had the strongest repercussions, was the loss of the family unit. Just a century ago, African-American families did not exist, and loyalty to a woman or child was disallowed. Our men were rewarded for making babies they weren't allowed to keep. Our children were crops to be sold at the auctions, and our wives were whoever would bear the greatest harvest.

> *God creates different types of people, and all are His handiwork. Celebrate and delight in the differences.*

Then slavery ended and the freed slaves were home free. Or were they? Free to do what? They had no life skills. No fathers to teach their sons how to make a marriage work. No one knew what parental responsibility meant. Their children had never been theirs to keep; they were sold to the highest bidder. What was family to them? The only family they knew was the one they served.

Emancipated but incapacitated. It has been a slow recovery. Our men struggle, pained by the failed attempts to become husbands and fathers. Without role models to follow, they have no direction, no concept of how to behave. Men called "boy" all their lives were left with anger and shattered self-esteem, and this is the legacy they give to their sons: generations of rage, often acted out against the wives and children who are the least deserving but the most accessible.

Infidelity and promiscuity, child abuse and child neglect—these are the side effects of a terrible time in history. While the scars are deep and the pain ever present, it is important that we crawl beyond the past of injustices into the morning light of triumphant possibility. We need to remove the chains that were unlocked decades ago and find a way to build families on foundations strong enough to support future generations. We must educate ourselves, and not only in spite of our past, but because of our past, work harder to create and nurture a family unit that will act as a support system and safety net as we endeavor to attain success in every area of life.

The Secret Ingredient

So how do we overcome our past experiences? How do we combine our separate and unique perspectives and create a harmonious blend that is appealing, satisfying, and good for us? There is a very special ingredient called grace that must be added to the mix. It bandages the damaged souls of broken people and allows the defeated to develop winning strategies to escape their pasts. It gives strength to those who struggle to make functional what has historically been dysfunctional. Grace renews the heart and reconciles the troubles of a tortured spirit. It is kindness and forgiveness. It is the favor of God, and as He bestows it on us, we should in turn give it to those who need our compassion and love.

We are all broken, and we must learn to accept and then help mend the brokenness in others. In the Book of Hosea, God tells the prophet to marry Gomer, the prostitute. She is a promiscuous woman who disgraced herself and her family. She was abused and battered, she was tattered and torn. She was broken. She ran away from Hosea, but he still wanted her. He could have said, "This woman hurt me, she humiliated me, she failed me." He could have left her on the auction block. But instead he calls after her, "Gomer . . . my Beloved." He empties his pockets to redeem her. Hosea's name means "salvation," and he, and his grace, saves Gomer.

Hosea's undying love for Gomer's broken life should give hope to the most severely damaged among us that there is healing for the broken places in the human soul. If we are to have successful relationships that gradually develop wholeness, we must understand that we must love and extend grace to imperfect, flawed people. Let us follow Hosea's example. Let us follow the Lord. As He loves and accepts unconditionally us imperfect beings, so, too, should we love and accept each other.

Celebrate Your Differences

As I said, we are each unique. We come to our relationships with different perceptions and definitions. We could be experiencing the same thing, but how we see it depends on our perspective. It's like that story of the blind men who are asked to describe an elephant. One man goes up to the side of the beast and feels its flank. He describes the elephant as a wall. A second blind man walks up to the elephant and grabs its smooth, sharp tusk. He says, "This animal is like a spear." A third man approaches the elephant and happens to grasp his trunk. He describes the elephant as a snake. The fourth man feels the elephant's leg and likens the beast to a tree. The fifth man touches the ear and it reminds him of a fan, and the sixth grabs the tail and is convinced the animal is like a rope. One elephant, six men, six different definitions. It's all about perspective.

> *Eve was created in man, called out of man, and then presented to man. Together Adam and Eve, man and woman, are a picture of the wholeness of God.*

Similarly, my wife and I have two totally different definitions of Christmas. Of course, the real meaning of Christmas is to commemorate the birth of the Lord, but the day has become more commercial than commemorative, and with that commercialization has come various ideas of how it should be celebrated. My wife and I have totally different ways of celebrating. My wife delights in the scent of pine in the house, the sweet voice of Mahalia Jackson singing "Silent Night," and lights in all the windows and in all the trees in the yard. The more lights, the better.

I don't need any of that. I don't like to spend a lot of time or money to put something up that I will take down in sixty days. You need thousands of lights, and the strings always seem to get tangled, no matter how neatly you put them away the year before. And then, if one light burns out the entire string doesn't work, and you have to spend hours at the tedious task of trying to determine which bulb is the culprit. No sir, I don't need those lights. We never had them when I was a kid. No, back then Christmas was celebrated with good food, and lots of it. And that's how I think we should honor the birthday of Christ—with a meal fit for a king. Keep the lights but cook the food. Give me more food than any human could possibly eat. I want to eat so much that I have to lay down and take a nap, so that I can get up and eat again.

My wife and I have two different definitions of the same holiday. My wife's family stressed the decorations at Christmas, while my family rarely decorated for the holiday—they were too busy cooking! But when we came together, my wife and I had to combine our two definitions and make them work. So every year I devote an entire day to sorting the lights and hanging them up, and I make sure to never complain once. And without fail, we have the most scrumptious feast imaginable. My wife is a great cook and always turns out delicious fare, but on Christmas she outdoes herself.

Part of making a marriage—or any relationship, for that matter—work is accepting each other's differences. Within your family you must respect each other's unique perspective, and although you do not need to agree, you must always honor where the other person is coming from. It's all about compromise and not deeming your values to be better than anyone else's. Who am I to tell my wife her Christmas lights are silly? When I take the time to realize her delight in them and understand that it is rooted in childhood memories of her family's special tradition, I not only respect her desire to have lights, I want to go out of my way to make sure every light is hung just right. That's what a good relationship is about.

> *All of us bring baggage into our relationships. Unpack the bags together.*

It is sad to say, but I have found that Christians sometimes have the hardest time respecting others' different values. I have known people who, before they joined the Church, lived a riotous life—drinking, smoking pot, caught up in a worldly existence of immediate gratification and sensual pleasures. Then—bang!—they find God and everything changes. They have Bibles all over the house, Andraé Crouch plays on the stereo, and they go to church seven days a week. I am delighted they have found the right path, but they become hell-bent on dragging everyone along with them. And they won't associate with anyone who doesn't adopt their newfound values. They refuse to eat dinner over at their brother's house because he doesn't say grace before meals. They throw their son out because he listens to heavy-metal music. The family decomposes because they try to force their values on the people they love, and set boundaries that prohibit association with those who don't accept those values. What a terrible misuse of Christianity. It has become a tool for manipulation and control whereby families, instead of showing loved ones "the way," lead them straight out the door.

> *Teamwork requires a leader, a goal, and an agreement. The strength of the family is greatest when we all work together toward the same goals.*

You have heard it said many times before: Communication is the key to making any relationship work. You will never understand the uniqueness of your mate, or other family members, if you do not learn how to effectively communicate. And you need to be able to explain your own points of view if you want others to accept them. Talk about where you are coming from. Ask questions and listen to the answers. Talk about your differences and celebrate them. Work to understand what it is other people value and respect those values.

However, when teaching communication we often focus on what we should say, when it is equally important what is not said. If you told a person everything you thought, they would leave you. There are private parts of you. Maturity means that everything you think doesn't need to be said. Everything you think has not been thought through. Don't speak in anger; emotional outbursts result in hurtful comments you do not mean and will later regret. You also should be careful of what you say when you are tired. Exhaustion puts your guard down, and at such times thoughtless comments can slip out. Always wait until your judgment is clear and you can think things out before you speak.

Creating a Winning Team

Your family is like a team. You must work together in order to win. And as a team you can successfully tackle any problem and weather any storm. But the first thing you must overcome is the limitations of each team member. Each family member has certain assets and liabilities. This includes you, too. You're not perfect, and your role is not to act like a handyman and try to fix everyone. The secret to creating a strong team is blending each member's unique talents so that the liabilities are minimized.

Learn to compensate for each other's inability. We are better together than we are apart. Maybe your mate is a disaster in the kitchen. She has trouble even boiling water. She keeps a spotless house and has a garden that is the envy of the neighborhood, but when it comes to cooking she is all thumbs. Don't berate her for her inability. Don't mock her just because you've been cooking since you were old enough to reach the stove. Instead, take the vegetables she expertly grows and create a meal that showcases their flavors. Work together and let your individual talents complement one another.

Championship sports teams don't come in first place because they have the best players. They win because they know how to work together. A star quarterback isn't worth much if there is nobody to catch his passes. Likewise in basketball, where even the most dominant center needs a point guard to get him the ball. The best players are the ones who know their teammates' strengths and weaknesses and work with them so that the entire team shines.

Make allowances for realities. Some people will never change. Learn to accept this. You could waste years complaining, causing rifts in your relationships and driving yourself crazy, or you could adjust your expectations and be a lot happier. If you know that Cousin Suzie is lazy, don't call her when you need help setting up that important dinner party. Call someone else whom you can depend on. When you learn to accept realities and make allowances, your home life will be harmonious and your relationships will thrive.

Are you serious about creating a winning team? Are you willing to put in the time and effort? Are you willing to be patient, tolerant, and adaptable? Your family might not be ideal, but it can be a source of support, resilience, and love, seeing you through a lifetime of experiences—the good and the bad. Invest in your family and you will reap the benefits of a winning team.

Sow Some Seed

The principle of the power of compounding, understood by the farmer and the financial investor, needs to be understood in our family relationships. If you invest in your relationships and sow good seed, you will reap a pleasant harvest. If you neglect your relationships, you'll end up with a field full of weeds.

Investment means you must be prepared to wait for a return.

Most couples divorce because they do not have patience to wait for the long-term returns. The stock market dropped out recently, but I decided to keep my investments intact because I understand that the stock market goes up and down, and over the long term will likely show a profit. When you invest in a relationship, do so with the long term in mind. Relationships will fluctuate with ups and downs through the stages and ages of life. If you bail out when things are down, you will regret it once you are out. You may see the one you left eventually matured and changed. If only you had waited a little while longer. You may not get an immediate return from a relationship, but what you sow you will reap in time.

The same is true for being a parent. It is not easy raising children. They will put you through much heartache and often not appreciate your efforts, but if you stick by them, they will grow up to be fine adults.

> *Train up a child in the way he should go: and when he is old, he will not depart from it.*
>
> PROVERBS 22:6 (KJV)

The passage doesn't say when "old" is or when the return will come. But if you stick with it long enough, God will bring glory in your life.

I wasn't a bad child, but I know I gave my mother her share of gray hairs. Sometimes I did well in school, other times I was in trouble. One day it seemed I was destined for success, and the next my mother would wonder how I would end up. Still, no matter what I put her through, she was always there for me. She gave me the best of her attention, wisdom, and resources. She supported all that I endeavored to do and was always in my corner. She invested her life in me, my brothers, and my sisters. And thus, it was only right that when she got older and had to have several major surgeries, when in the last few years of her life she struggled with Alzheimer's disease, that she came to live with me so that I could care for her. She had that return coming to her, and I was glad to do it. I tried to do whatever was required to make her comfortable. She had invested so much in me and got so little return when I was still a child. The greatest return came when it was needed most, in the later years of her life.

Family relationships are long-term investments. They require much work and vigilant care. But the returns are invaluable. The one who blesses you the most may not always be the one who reflected or agreed with your religious views, married a husband you approved of, or invited you over for dinner. Don't sweat the small stuff. In the long run it won't matter. What does matter is that you tend to your family now and nurture a team that is mutually supportive and constantly loving. Make the investment in your family, and together enjoy the fruits of your harvest.

7.

Intimacy Means
Into-me-see

In any discussion of family, we must talk about the family we choose, the family we build from scratch. I am referring to the union of two separate souls, coming together to blend their pasts and create a future. I am referring to marriage.

Marriage is a major commitment. Think of what marriage is. You are giving yourself to another person. What could you give a person that is more important than yourself? You are investing your life in hopes that you will reap the reward of a lifelong partner who will remain by your side in good times and in bad. Such a monumental step, yet every day so many close their eyes, march forward, and take the leap.

One hopes that these love-sick couples take the time to contemplate the ramifications of the decision they are about to make. Can they distance themselves from the emotional and sexual urges that intoxicate them and rationally determine if they are ready to make this investment, till death do them part? Do they really know the person they are about to be bound to? Do they really know themselves?

For most, before they have had time to really grapple with these questions, the invitations are sent out and the aunts and uncles have flown in to witness the exchange of vows. The vows are straight-forward and fairly simple to articulate. The struggle is not to say them but to live them for a lifetime. Have the man and woman who stand before the altar thought about what they really mean? Or are they just caught up in a moment, try-ing to live out a scene they once saw in a movie? The problem is that this is not Hollywood. The bride and the groom may be acting out their part perfectly for the moment, but there is no director who will yell, "Cut!" This is a live-action drama— no second takes and no rehearsals.

> *He who finds a wife finds a good thing, and obtains favor from the LORD.*
>
> PROVERBS 18:22
>
> (NKJV)

Too often, the pageantry of the ceremony overshadows the magnitude of the commitment. The caterer's menu becomes more important than the promise made before God. Couples worry about what to wear and whom to invite, when in reality they should be standing with naked souls before each other. And so, like sleepwalkers, they take the step and free-fall into their future.

The preacher, with his rich baritone voice, leads them through the ceremony with the experience of a maître d' escort-ing a couple through a fine restaurant. He has done this many times. Sometimes it works, and other times the couple ends up in his office angry and frustrated, disappointed and aggravated. Each time he asks them if they will live out their vows for as long as they both shall live. But how can they answer that? Who can say with total assurance what they will and will not do? Who knows what tomorrow will bring? Can they say with complete confidence that they are ready to walk through the unforeseen with the unknown to an undetermined location for an undisclosed period of time? Yet they clear their throats, and loudly and distinctly proclaim, "I do."

And it is done. "I now pronounce you man and wife," says the preacher. The mothers cry, the veil is removed, and the promise is sealed in a kiss.

Coming Together

Later, when the guests are gone and the couple is alone, they will consummate the commitment in the marriage bed. And whether it is the first time for them or not, it is the first time on this side of the altar. In a blaze of passion their bodies meet, and as two become one, they begin their journey of what both hope will be wedded bliss.

As sacred as the sexual act is, it is not the most important thing that is happening this night. Most normal red-blooded boys and girls can figure out how to make their bodies connect. But they now face the challenge of trying to get their hearts to connect as well as their bodies do. How do I go about joining your past to his? How do you connect the weaknesses in you to

> *Be grateful and let your spouse know that you appreciate the things he or she does for the family.*

the weaknesses in her? How do you accommodate the secrets that will reveal themselves as you undress your souls before one another?

It is easier to wiggle out of the tightest clothes than to remove the layers of history that drape your souls. You have hidden beneath them for so long, and to stand naked is to stand vulnerable. But you must unveil your scars and reveal your broken pasts. You must show each other where your hurt is, or else it will fester between you like an undetected cancer and eat away at your potential future. In marriage you should find a safe place and a safe person with whom you can be transparent.

A Perfect Fit

And Adam said, This is now bone of my bones, and flesh of my flesh: she shall be called Woman, because she was taken out of Man.

Therefore shall a man leave his father and his mother, and shall cleave unto his wife: and they shall be one flesh.

GENESIS 2:23–24 (KJV)

The very first marriage was the reuniting of a man and the woman who had existed within his own body. They were one before, and they became one again. A careful consideration of these lines gives you the Designer's plan for the perfect union. The implication is that when a man and a woman come together in a marriage they complete each other and become whole. They shall be of one flesh. This is not just sexual coupling. The physical stimulation is just the tip of the iceberg; what's really orgasmic is finding the missing part of your self.

When you come together in marriage, you are no longer just a man and woman. You are a couple, a unit. And the total is greater than the sum of its parts. You become one, working together, surviving together, thriving together.

What a wonderful plan for marriage. How did we get so far away from what God had in mind when He created us? His plan was perfect—a pattern for a seamless garment. What went wrong? There is nothing wrong with the plan, but today, the material we have to work with is likely flawed and damaged. We have the challenge of taking the damaged material and producing a happy life. How do we do this? The Bible offers us a pattern for a union that is perfect, holy, pure, and sublime. Then we roll over and look at the reality. How do we reconcile the difference between the ideal and the real?

The Ideal

And he shall take a wife in her virginity.

A widow, or a divorced woman, or profane, or an harlot, these shall he not take: but he shall take a virgin of his own people to wife.

Neither shall he profane his seed among his people: for I the LORD do sanctify him.

LEVITICUS 21:13–15 (KJV)

The instructions are quite clear: both man and woman should enter into matrimony pure and untouched. I believe God knew that the experiences of our past would affect the expectations of our future. He knew that excess baggage of past experiences would undermine the success of a relationship. It was His design that there be a sense of purity and newness associated with the relationship. Can you imagine how freeing it would be to have no comparisons? One couldn't compare this man to another. She could not be judged in relationship to another woman. There would be no expectations; it would be a new experience for both of them.

The definition of marriage would begin there in the marital bed. The two would come together, naked in body and soul, and consummate the union in the sexual act. Soft words would be spoken, blood would be split, and two hearts would meet in the night. Marriage was meant to be the strongest possible of covenants, and it would be sealed with blood.

> *When a woman appreciates what her husband does, she is, in essence, appreciating him. His self-esteem is often tied to what he does. Attack it and you have attacked him.*

The blood covenant was taken very seriously. According to the Bible, the life of the flesh is in the blood, and it is the blood that makes atonement for the soul (Leviticus 17:11, NKJV). The blood on the bridal sheets is the ultimate offering the bride and groom could make to seal their lifelong oath of commitment. Both are offering their lives for the sake of the union.

In essence, Leviticus 17:11 underscores the preferred plan of absolute purity as necessary—not an option—for the ideal relationship. It is sad that we don't teach this early on, as it would cause both women and men to value their bodies and the power of giving it to someone. Leviticus also renounces deceitfulness, which often destroys a marriage more than anything else. If we hide our past from each other, we hide ourselves. Intimacy means telling the truth about who you are, where you've been, and scaling the walls together toward the common goal of a lifelong relationship. The blood is symbol for the covenant, trust, and innocent surrender.

> *If a man takes a wife and, after lying with her, dislikes her and slanders her and gives her a bad name, saying, "I married this woman, but when I approached her, I did not find proof of her virginity," then the girl's father and mother shall bring proof that she was a virgin to the town elders at the gate. . . . If, however, the charge is true and no proof of the girl's virginity can be found, she shall be brought to the door of her father's house and there the men of her town shall stone her to death. She has done a disgraceful thing in Israel by being promiscuous while still in her father's house. You must purge the evil from among you.*
>
> DEUTERONOMY 22:13–21 (NIV)

If the bride was not pure, she might be stoned to death. By the standards of Old Testament virtue, there might be quite a heap of stones beside many hotels today! But this was the original idea. It was one of the purest and deepest commitments. Marriage born out of this kind of wedding, consummated by the blood of the bride, was the ideal. The two would come together and remain so for the rest of their lives.

> *Your wife doesn't want to be the runner-up. Your woman needs to know that she is at the top of your list, above your career and not a runner-up to it.*

Had this book been written twenty years ago during the sexual revolution, secular minds would have scoffed at the antiquated ideas of the Master's plan. But since sexually transmitted diseases have caused the deaths of so many promiscuous people, even the atheist is adopting a similar view of monogamy. For all of us are forced to live with the tragic consequences of human frailties and inconsistencies. Now there is a convergence of thought between the spiritual and the secular. Now even those who had been ready to abolish the whole idea of marriage are rethinking the institution, or at least being more discriminating in their choice of sexual partners. The stones of the Old Testament have become the plagues of this generation. I am not sure which is more deadly, the stones of men or the body stoning itself with infections and incurable diseases.

Let's Get Real

In any case, the ideal was monogamy, and that is what we should all aspire to today. But the fact that the diseases are spreading and vows are broken testifies that we are far from the ideal. Although we should enter marriage pure and inexperienced, the sad reality is that more often than not, we have had multiple experiences— some willingly, some forced upon us. Tragically, many couples today are not waving bloodstained sheets after the wedding night. The stains that they wave are battle scars from the past. They are the tearstained pillowcases. They are the cloaks of unresolved issues they wrap around themselves to protect their souls from further damage.

Before we reach the altar, we've had a lifetime of circumstances that affect how we define love, sex, and intimacy. World-wise and -weary, we enter the marriage chamber and carry with us baggage too

Instead of focusing on your mate's weaknesses or your own, focus on the strength of God to restore your marriage.

heavy to bear alone, but too painful to share. Weighted down with these burdens, we climb into bed, dragging our pasts along with us. And even a king-sized bed gets too cramped when our histories, expectations, and broken dreams lie beside us.

In my twenty-three years as a counselor, I have spoken with countless couples as they approach their wedding day, and the expectations they bring with them are unbelievable. And I have found that it is not only their experiences that color their expectations, but also a combination of barbershop bragging, beauty parlor ramblings, and television dramas that give rise to a conglomerate of ideas that have no basis in reality. They look at marriage through lenses formed by all the places they've been, all that they've done, and the people they've met along the way.

Now, as a Christian, I espouse the ideal put forth by my Maker in the most holy of manuals, the Bible. As a preacher, I encourage my congregation to be pure in body, mind, and spirit. But as I stand at the pulpit and look out into the faces of the people who fill our churches, I must be a realist. As a servant of God, I must minister to those in need. I can encourage ideals, but I must operate in the realm of reality. It is important to help the pure remain pure, but there is a great deal of material devoted to the teaching of Christian virtue. Instead, I would like to talk to those who find themselves in their second or third marriage. I would like to address the so-called "real people" who have had secret experiences, molestations, traumas, abuses, and early promiscuities. It is to them that I direct this message, for they will need constant care in order to rebuild what life has torn away from them.

Happily ever after is found in children's storybooks, but not in many homes. The majority of people are scarred and damaged. They struggle to make the ideal work within the limitation of their realities. Our lack of instruction to them has not helped their cause. Our silence to them has left them adrift in a sea of escalating divorce rates and broken hearts. Well, I say it is time to throw them a lifeline. It is time to break the silence and be real.

As we stand on the threshold of the twenty-first century, our challenge as Christians is to maintain our commitment to God's standards and ideals while building a bridge whereby faith and biblical wisdom will become accessible to those who are steeped in reality. The only way we can do this is to season our ideals with the grace of God. If we fail to do this, we fail a generation. We lose them and leave them feeling hopelessly left out. We need to realize where they are coming from, and only then can we show them the way.

Putting the Pieces Together

Many of us are damaged. Like the clay spoken about in Jeremiah 18, we are marred. But God, in His infinite good grace, allows us the opportunity to mend in His hands. He applies His touch and stretches us beyond our past so that we can have a successful future. And He wants us to find someone we can share this future with. So we wait for Mr. Right or Ms. Outta Sight. And we wait, and we wait. We wait as our frustrations grow and we begin to doubt that there is anyone out there for us.

So you decide to have a little fun with Mr. Okay For Now and you wind up hurt and confused. You spend some time with Ms. Too Good To Be True until you discover she is, and she leaves you with a broken heart and an empty wallet. Mr. Almost and Ms. Pretty Close come along, but the more you get to know them, the farther from the ideal they seem. They're not perfect, but if you are really honest with yourself, neither are you.

Life is very much like a puzzle, and we are the pieces that have fallen to the floor. Some of the pieces have been stepped on; some have been lost for a while, carelessly kicked under the couch. But amid these oddly shaped fragments, there are two that fit each other. They do not fit because they are perfect. They fit because they are perfect for each other. They fit because the odd shape of one nests perfectly in the curvature of the other. Apart they are two pieces without any definition, but when they come together they complement each other and take on meaning.

> *Let the Holy Spirit be your Marriage Counselor. He is the Chemist that gives you and your companion chemistry. Seek Him for understanding.*

This is the joy of a marriage. It is not the celebration of legal sex. It is not being able to file joint tax returns and claim deductions. It is the coming together of two damaged souls lost on the sea of reality. They drifted far from the ideal, but when they find each other and embrace, they become mutual life preservers, keeping each other afloat. I can see them now, looking like small bubbles in the midst of the raging sea. They hold on to each other, two lovers, a mother and a father, making love and making babies, and making each other feel complete. And in fact, together they are ideal.

I beseech all of you to recognize the brokenness in you and courageously strip off the tough exterior you use to hide your pain. Expose yourself to your partner, be transparent, and let honesty define your union. Be accepting of your spouse's uniqueness and honor your differences. Let the grace of God enter your life and your marriage so that you and your mate can come together, be one, and walk as children of God: whole, complete, and fulfilled.

Lord,

I have found my friend for life. My soul mate, my partner. I love not for sex, nor need, but because in spite of my failures, I have found someone that fits with me. My rib, my missing link. I thank You that I didn't drown in the sea of my mistakes, nor die gasping beneath the weight of guilt over things I could not change. But You, in all Your grace, have crafted someone who fits the misfit in me. In the vast ocean of humanity, You have enabled me to find my mate.

Father, give me the courage to expose who I am and remain transparent to the one with whom I am joined in holy matrimony. Today I stretch wide my soul, strip off my inhibitions, and with faith in Your purpose, reach out to the one I love and say, "Into-me-see." Amen.

8.

My Family Is
My Team

Not all families are the same. However, regardless of a family's configuration, it can still be a team, a unit, a mighty force in the face of crisis, and an unbeatable source of love and support. A family can be a team without a mother or father; a family can be grandparents raising grandchildren. Perhaps you and your spouse each had children from previous marriages. This blending of broods can be challenging, but with some care and planning, the result can be a successful merger. There may not even be a romantic element to your family. Maybe it's just you and your sister sharing an apartment. Or possibly it's you, and Cousin Ellen, and Uncle Tyrone and his two daughters from his first marriage.

Although it would be ideal to have a father and mother and two children in one house with two sets of grandparents who visit on the holidays, you must learn to work with the reality that you wake up to each morning. You must stop seeing yourself as a statistic in someone's study of the failure of the traditional American family, and begin to view yourself as a team, with a unique combination of players. But to function successfully as a team, you need a strategy based on the uniqueness of your situation.

All teams, no matter how great the individual players, need to learn how to operate as a unit. They need a strategy that will help them maximize their strengths and minimize their liabilities. The same holds true for your family. You need to look at the reality of your situation and then act in such a way that will offset any deficits.

No Help, No Mate, and Children

Sometimes a family is a woman raising kids by herself, bringing home the bacon and cooking it, too. Through death, divorce, or pregnancy out of wedlock, these women find themselves the one adult in a household of children. They are responsible for paying the bills, disciplining the children, going to PTA meetings, and coaching Little League. They are trying to be both mother and father. But no matter how diligent they are, no matter how loving, no matter that they are doing a phenomenal parenting job in less than an ideal situation, the fact remains that there is a lack of a male presence in the house.

To compensate for this deficit, the mother should take steps to expose her children to male role models. Young boys need to be around men who can be positive influences, who can act as a prototype they can aspire to. It is just as important for daughters to have a male presence in the home. Without it, she will pine after masculine love but not understand a man when she gets married. She will find herself used and abused by men because of her need to receive the adoration, affection, and male love that she never had when she was a child.

Now, I'm not saying that single mothers should indiscriminately bring every Tom, Dick, and Harry into the house and the lives of her children. Much more harm than good will come from providing inappropriate role models. It should go without saying that physically, emotionally, and sexually abusive men should not be allowed to cross the threshold of your home. But you should also be aware of the messages the men in your life impart to your children. Young minds are like sponges, soaking up everything they hear and see. Does he swear and talk disrespectfully about women? Is that behavior you want your son to emulate? Does he lie on the couch all day while you work, doing the cooking, the cleaning, and the laundry besides? Do you want your daughter to think a woman should provide maid ser-

> *Have a vision and purpose for your family. Set and achieve specific goals each year.*

vice just so she can have a man around—no matter how lazy he is? Expose your children to male role models, but make sure the men are worth modeling.

Although single fathers are a less common phenomenon, I address this same advice to men. Both boys and girls need female influence in their lives. There are some things girls can learn about only from a woman. Your daughter needs female companionship, someone to confide in, and someone she can pattern herself after as she grows into womanhood. Boys, too, need to have a feminine influence in their lives. They need to learn how to treat and interact with women so that they will grow up to be loving and respectful men.

Single parents, don't let television characters or sports figures be the role models your children look up to and seek to emulate. Introduce to your children people who embody the values you want them to embrace. Turn to your extended family and your friends, go to your church or local Big Brother/Big Sister organization, and find men and women who are like the men and women you want your children to grow up to be.

Mix and Match

Single parents are sometimes fortunate enough to find a good man or woman, fall in love, and marry. However, they now face the challenge of taking two separate families—the one they had with their children and the new one they created in the sacrament of holy matrimony—and combining them in such a way as to create a team that serves all members. This feat may be doubly difficult if the new mate has children of his or her own.

The merger is a challenging undertaking in and of itself, but add visiting rights, custodial care, court intervention, and ex–in–law intervention and you have a situation that could be more complicated than negotiating an international peace treaty. You need to plow through piles of paperwork, follow legal specifications, and always keep first and foremost what is best for the children.

Do you take these children to be your brothers and sisters, for better or for worse, for richer or for poorer? Do you promise to accept this new mom or dad as your own, keeping ties with your biological parent yet obeying your stepparent on a day-to-day basis? Do you promise to share your toys that your father bought you with this new child who happens to be the child of the man your mother just married? These are the questions that would be asked if there was a ceremony that united families. These are the questions that *should* be asked when you attempt to blend families. You can't just throw your children together and say, "Play nice." You can't just turn their world up-side down. You must allow them time to digest a situation that is difficult to digest. You must give them time to adjust, and acknowledge that they are struggling to make sense of something that is complex and confusing for even the adults involved. You need to prepare yourselves and the children for the changes. You must talk and listen, and have a plan so that this merger can be as painless and stress-free as possible.

> *Spend quality time with your children. Your time is the most valuable gift you can give.*

Big Momma's House

In many households, especially in the African-American community, we find grandmothers raising their children's children. Lovingly called "Big Momma," these women who have spent years rearing their own children now find themselves changing diapers and burping babies for the second time. They may have thought their job as parents was done, but many are forced into situations where they have to intervene so that their grandbaby can have a home. These remarkable women value family so highly that they willingly take on the responsibility of raising children that are not their own. But then again, to these women the children are theirs; they are part of the family, part of the team. And although arthritis may cripple these women's hands and age may weaken their arms, they will do all they can to hold their family together.

There is much to admire about families such as these. They are situations less of obligation and more of appreciation— appreciation for what family is and means. The women who run these households give selflessly, and they certainly have much to give. Generally, they are seasoned women whose conflicts have been resolved years before, and many find a certain sense of purpose in the children that they keep. These women are often more maternal and have a wealth of previous parenting experience. And they have the wisdom that only age can bring to impart to the young charges in their care.

But there are disadvantages to this type of family. It takes an enormous amount of energy to chase a toddler or keep up with an adolescent. It is difficult to run behind a tricycle when your joints ache or deal with teenage rebellion when your patience has been worn thin by advanced age. And even if you are a youthful, vital sixty-five years old now, when your little charge hits adolescence you will be eighty, and by the time he

> Attend church together as a family, and have family devotions or Bible study.

goes to college you may very well be dead and gone. I am not saying older people can't parent, but it is so much easier when you are in your youth.

Another disadvantage is that although these grandmothers know a lot about parenting, much of that information is dated.

Times were different when they raised their children, and they may be preparing their grandchildren for a day that no longer exists. Societal roles and pressures have changed dramatically over just the last ten years. Children today are exposed to so much on television and on the Internet. They are wise beyond their years with information not necessarily suitable for, or able to be processed by, young minds. Our youth today are far more advanced than those of a generation ago. Things are so different that grandmothers may feel as if they are first-time mothers again. It's challenging enough bringing up children, but if a generation gap as wide as the Grand Canyon separates you, the job is that much tougher.

To all of you grandmothers rearing your grandchildren, I tip my hat to you. Your commitment to family is admirable. Your family structure may not be ideal, but you are holding it together and making it work. However, you owe it to yourselves and the children you are raising to understand your strengths and limitations. Become familiar with the challenges and temptations that children of this generation will face outside your home and protective care. And like the single mother, look for the outside resources and influences that are necessary to make up for your limitations. Take a realistic look at the years you have before you and make a plan to compensate for the toll time and raising a grandbaby will have on your health and energy. As your grandbaby gets older, so do you. Take care of the child's needs by taking care of your own.

I applaud all the families out there who are making it through the maze of life effectively, who are functioning as a team in spite of obvious limitations or obstacles. Develop a strategy for success based on your unique situation and the challenges you must face, and your family will thrive. Your efforts are testimony to the strength, resilience, and determination family can provide.

Create the Vision

Regardless of your family's makeup, there are certain things you must do to create a winning team. First of all, every team needs a coach. No matter how talented the individual players may be, without the guidance and leadership of a coach, even all-stars will look like the Bad News Bears.

If you are reading this book, chances are that you care enough about your family to take the responsibility to be the coach. It's not always an easy job. You have to be an adult; you have to be mature. Your days of tantrums are over. Your days of waking up in the morning and not going to work simply because you don't feel like it are over. Your days of leaving your team to fend for itself because you want to go out and party are over. You must grow up.

> *Raising children requires that you listen at least as much as you talk. Encourage as well as critique.*

Now, probably the most important job of a coach is to create a vision for your team. What does this mean? It means you must define for your team their purpose, their mission statement. What is the purpose of your family? What values will it exemplify? What code will it live by? What will you do with the resources, talent, and skill that each member brings to the table? What will you do with what God has given you?

Psalms 127:4 compares children to arrows in the quiver of a

mighty man: "Like arrows in the hand of a warrior, so are the children of one's youth" (NKJ). This means our children have to be aimed like an arrow, directed toward a goal. As a parent, you have to have your hand on the bow. This is part of your job as family leader. You need to aim that bow and shoot those arrows as far as you can, using all the strength that God has given you. You must give your children direction and purpose. You must aim your child toward goals and help them reach them.

But in order to give anyone direction, you must have it yourself. What is your purpose? Do you live it out every single day? Does every action you commit, every person you bring into your life, lead you in the direction you want to go? If you want to find a life partner and a father for your children who will love and care for you and lead your family to excellence, why are you hanging around with that good-for-nothing, abusive bum? If you want to create a prosperous future for you and your children, why are you squandering your weekly paycheck on fast food and fancy clothes, instead of investing it in a mutual fund that will yield high interest and help you attain your financial dreams? You need to determine where you want to go and then take steps to get there. You can't lead your family anywhere if you don't know where you are going.

The Huddle

To lead your team effectively, you need to regularly get together in a huddle. The huddle is where you discuss your strategy. It is where you set your financial goals, discuss the division of responsibilities, and tackle other issues that will determine the success or failure of your team. For Christians, prayer is an essential part of the huddle and an invaluable asset. But even the most powerful prayers will not be able to overcome the challenges of family life by prayer alone. Prayer unifies the team and turns to the Divine for guidance. However, although the strategy may come from overhead, the plays must be accomplished on the field. There must be a huddle whereby the feeling of team effort erupts and everyone agrees on how to execute the plan. Agreement is essential. For only when you agree can you make things happen.

> *Again I say unto you, That if two of you shall agree on earth as touching any thing that they shall ask, it shall be done for them of my Father which is in heaven.*
>
> MATTHEW 18:19 (KJV)

To have agreement you must have a huddle. You must come together and work through issues, talk through disagreements and differences, and reach an agreement. You need to talk and listen. It is not the job of the coach to talk and everyone to listen. You may be the head of the house, but that doesn't mean you are the only one who can think or has a valid opinion. You may have to make the final decision, but each member of your team should be part of the decision-making process. Letting everyone contribute is acknowledging that everyone plays a role in the family and is partly responsible for its success or failure.

> *Know when to lessen your grip; as your children develop more maturity, release more responsibility into their hands.*

Listening is an essential element of good leadership. When

you listen with an open heart, you learn to understand how your team members think and feel. This is important. They will not cooperate, they will not work as a cohesive unit, if they do not feel that they are a part of a team and their needs are being met. Sure, you can rule with an iron fist and act like the Gestapo enforcing your will, but sooner or later you will face a mutiny. Resentment builds when people feel left out.

The family isn't a dictatorship. You can't just tell everyone what they have to do and when they have to do it. No, as coach, your job is to look to each member of the family, consider their input, listen to their views, and incorporate it all into a plan that serves the purpose of the entire unit. It's about leading your team members and encouraging them to be the best they can be so that the entire family can soar.

There are always forces working against you, undermining your efforts to achieve cohesive agreement. It seems as though Satan himself sends discord and pettiness as weapons to subvert the unity of family you are trying to create. Beware of selfishness and shortsightedness. Look beyond what you want, to what is in the best interest of the family as a unit. Don't fall under the spell of instant gratification. Sometimes what seems good today takes you off the path of a better tomorrow.

Also be wary of kitchen-table counselors who meddle where they don't belong and fuel the tensions that can destroy your team. Avoid counseling from those not qualified to do so. If you need help, seek a trained professional, a clergyman, someone whose advice is based on more than mere opinion and personal experience.

Don't let outsiders into your huddle. Respect the privacy of

Family traditions started early in the life of the family give the family identity and keep the family together.

team members by not disclosing family issues to others. Your next-door neighbor, the lady down the street, and Uncle Jimmy's barber have no place in your huddle. They have no right to offer opinions on issues that don't concern them. In fact, their opinions are worthless, for they are usually based on hearsay, self-interest, or jealousy.

Communicate with those on your team. I have met with people who say they can talk to outsiders more easily than they can family members. This is a shame. And it is dangerous, for it stops you from developing the skills necessary to work with the people who really impact your life. When it comes right down to it, it is your family that pulls together and helps you survive a crisis, overcome health challenges, and pick yourself back up when you fall to pieces.

Draw your family together into a huddle regularly. Talk and listen and seek to come to agreement, so that your team will be one body, working together to achieve success.

. . . walk worthy of the calling with which you were called, with all lowliness and gentleness, with longsuffering, bearing with one another in love, endeavoring to keep the unity of the Spirit in the bond of peace.

EPHESIANS 4:1–3 (NKJV)

Pride in the Past and the Present

Another key to developing a winning team is to celebrate your family's heritage. Every family has a history that is rich and full of achievements. Every family has strengths that are unique and distinctive. These strengths may well be responsible for the life you enjoy today. Honor your family's past by celebrating it in the present. I am not necessarily talking about erecting monuments to commemorate your ancestors' accomplishments. The greatest tribute you could pay your relatives is to lovingly remember their contributions, and to emulate their ways so that their gifts live on.

Sharing your heritage with your team accomplishes several things. It creates a sense of pride and gives self-esteem to all the members. To acknowledge that you share a strong legacy encourages everyone to live up to the standards set by those before them. Let your family's past serve as a foundation upon which to build future achievement. A sense of history can inspire a desire to perpetuate the greatness.

In recent years in the church, we have preached much about generational curses. It is time that we begin to actively pass on generational blessings to our children. And every family has them. You don't need a million dollars or a Nobel Peace Prize to bestow an inheritance on your children. You need to pass on the values, wisdom, and love that got your family to where it is today. You need to tell them how you made it over your Jordan River and into your Promised Land. You must pass on to them the recipe of life that served your family well for years.

However, while it is important to celebrate your family's heritage, it is also necessary to point out each team member's individual and unique gifts. There is something in each person that makes them stand out from all others. We all have special talents, and all of us are interested in hearing what we do well. Yes, there are times when we must reprimand, but sometimes we are so generous with our criticism and so vague with our compliments. We need to recognize and verbalize the uniqueness of each player. We need to emphasize that although we belong to a great team, we are not restricted by our heritage; we have the freedom and the ability to exercise our own individual gifts.

Honor your shared heritage, but celebrate each other's uniqueness. Enable your family to be proud of where they came from, where they are, and where they can go. Our past binds us together, but it is every member utilizing his or her special gifts and fulfilling a particular role that makes a family strong.

Hover

> In the beginning God created the heavens and the earth. The earth was without form, and void: and darkness was on the face of the deep. And the Spirit of God was hovering over the face of the waters.
>
> GENESIS 1:1–2 (NKJV)

Before God's creation was complete, He hovered. Although everything was in chaos, He was nearby and in control. To hover is to stay nearby and watch over. It's like a mother hen that broods over a nest of eggs, waiting for them to hatch. Know that the Holy Spirit hovers over your life as well.

But you, too, must hover. You must wait and watch and protect and nourish while the things in your life hatch. Your marriage needs to hatch. It starts out as two impassioned lovers joining together in a fairy-tale dream and needs to hatch into a long-lasting relationship built on friendship, trust, love, and respect. You need to hover while it hatches. Your children need to be hatched from childhood into maturity. You need to hover.

Hatching takes time. If unborn greatness is going to be incubated and delivered, expect the process to take time. So you have to patiently hover. Stop looking for immediate gratification. Don't try to step in and make things happen before their time. Have faith and hover. In Genesis 1:1–3, the earth was in a chaotic state. Maybe your family seems chaotic. Please know that chaos is curable; you just need to hover and let the hatching take place.

Keep in mind that not all eggs hatch at the same time. Not all marriages mature at the same speed. Not all children develop at the same pace. All of us who have raised children know what it is like to be anxious for your child to speak or be potty trained. We wonder and worry, but all parenting experts say, leave your children alone. They will speak when they are ready. Unless there is a serious medical problem, sooner or later they will learn to use the toilet. Each case is unique. As a parent, you just have to wait and hover.

In the same way, we are often anxious to see the miracle of teamwork happen in our family as quickly as it did for someone else. Rest assured, if you apply the principles set forth herewith, your team will develop. It might not happen tomorrow; it might not happen the same way it did for the Jones family down the street. But keep working toward your goal. Start to change your thinking. Instead of "If things don't get better, I'm leaving," develop the thought "I'm in this for the long term because I have too much invested to let it go. I'm going to sit on my team until there is a hatching." In most cases, if you hover until the hatching, great things will be born.

Lord, Save My House

God told Moses that the angel of death would come and destroy all the firstborn males in Egypt. But God made a provision for the children of Israel. He said to kill an animal and take its lifeblood and spread it on the doorposts and lintels of their houses.

You need to cover your team with blood to protect them. What do I mean by this? You simply pray that the blood of Jesus will cover their hearts, minds, spirits, and bodies. It doesn't matter how bad they are—cover them with the blood of Jesus. The blood of the Lamb is a biblical reference to Christ dying on the cross to save us.

You may have often asked God to save you, but what about your family? What about your marriage and your affection toward each other? Right now, say a prayer: "Dear Jesus, save my love for my family. Save their love for me. Don't let the railing winds of tempestuous times blow out the candle of our affection toward each other. Dear Lord, save my house."

Whatever else you may be able to do for your family, prayer is the most significant. Christ's blood prayed daily over your family will keep the destroyer at bay and away from your team. If you fail to pray and cover your family, through prayer, in Jesus' blood, you leave them open to potential spiritually destructive influences that can tear the family apart.

Take the time and put in the effort to make your family your team. Develop a game plan, learn to work together, and practice, practice, practice. Cooperate to maximize your strengths, minimize your liabilities, and learn to function as a unit. The bell has sounded, the game has begun, your team is up at bat. Take your plan and build on your years of practice; play hard, play fair, and most important, play as a team and as the champions you shall be.

9

Help, My House Is Out of Control

All of us have radios in our homes and cars. And at any given time, on any particular day, we may have our radios set on the same station, listening to the same song as everyone else, but with the radio set at different volumes. The emotional intensity levels in our homes are similar to the volume of the radio. The same events that occur in one home often occur in others. But people react to things differently. So many of us experience the same events; we encounter the same challenges and disappointments. Yet some people react reasonably and others respond with an emotional ten.

In homes where the volume is set high, there is always a crisis. The first time a husband and wife have a disagreement, they are headed to divorce court. A child misses curfew by five minutes? Look out for World War III.

I know that some of you know exactly what I'm talking about. You respond to life in extremes. The people at work have seen you explode; you've been known to slip into rage mode while waiting in line at the bank. And let's not even talk about how you behave when you're behind the wheel of a car. You confront the same life issues that everyone else does, but the difference is in how you react—or better said, how you overreact.

> But now is the time to get rid of anger, rage, malicious behavior, slander and dirty language.
> COLOSSIANS 3:8
> (NLT)

You need to control your emotions; don't let them control you. I'm not saying you should never get upset. We are only human, and things will occur that cause our blood to boil. But you need to be selective about what upsets you. What really matters? You may like your eggs cooked a certain way, but if they're a bit too runny, is it worth starting a fight over? Children need to abide by rules and guidelines, and to be disciplined when they misbehave. But there is a difference between punishment that instructs and punishment that destructs. Flying off the handle at the slightest thing will only push your children away and build a wall between you that is not easily torn down.

Your extreme behavior also affects your children in another way. Your emotional outbursts will infect the entire home. Children mirror their parents' behavior. If they are raised in a house that is consistently on high volume, they will react similarly. Your actions are training them to be hysterical and violent. Soon everyone will be overreacting, flying into fits of rage at the drop of a hat. You will be attacking each other, and when a team attacks its own members, it falls apart and is incapable of winning.

> *Any kingdom divided against itself will be ruined, and a house divided against itself will fall.*
>
> LUKE 11:17B (NIV)

In truth, when you exhibit tantrumlike behavior, you are acting out of a selfish, impatient need to get what you want, when you want it, in the way you think you ought to have it. Start behaving like an adult and exhibit self-control. You must have faith and patience. You will not gain the benefits of a strong, loving family if you cannot stand delayed gratification. As I've already stated, your family is a long-term investment. Put the time in now, and you will reap the benefits when you need them most.

Lower the volume in your house. You might not be able to control what happens in life, but you can control how you react to it. Weather the inevitable storms that come your way by staying focused on your family vision. Do you want a household that blares with the incoherent racket of everybody screaming and yelling and overacting? Or do you want a team that works together harmoniously? Set the tone in your home. Lower the volume and bring peace into your home.

Anger in the Bosom

Be not hasty in thy spirit to be angry: for anger resteth in the bosom of fools.

ECCLESIASTES 7:9 (KJV)

Because our personal volume is set too high, many of us talk to each other without thinking. We let our emotions dictate our reactions, and oftentimes we say things in the heat of the moment that we don't necessarily mean. The problem is that although words seem fleeting, heated words burn into the minds and souls of people they are directed to. Our wrath may pass like a summer storm, but it can leave a trail of bitterness and pain.

Children are most vulnerable to our angry outbursts. They are easy targets and unfortunately are often the innocent victims of misdirected rage. A man is frustrated with his job; he does too much, gets paid too little, and has to deal with the inequities of a mismanaged work environment. He can't yell at his boss; he can't quit his job. He comes home like a volcano ready to erupt. No sooner does he walk through the door than he is spewing his venomous anger at anyone who crosses his path. He yells at his daughter for spilling some milk; his son is yanked out of a chair and sent to his room because the television is too loud. He slams the door as he storms out of the house because dinner isn't cooked the way he likes it. He may have left the premises, but his anger has done its damage.

Even if anger is not specifically directed toward a person, it can infect your home. How many children have heard their mother rail against her man as she talks on the phone to her best girlfriend? "All men are dogs, girl; there's not a good one in the pack." These angry messages shape the way children view their daddy, and men and women in general. Daughters can inherit more than their mothers' eyes or hair; they can inherit their anger, and grow up never trusting or allowing themselves to be emotionally available to men. As a parent, God gave you clay when He gave you your child. Clay is to be molded and developed. You will shape your child's destiny by your words, behavior, and attitude.

> Simeon and Levi are brethren; instruments of cruelty are in their habitations. O my soul, come not thou into their secret; unto their assembly, mine honour, be not thou united: for in their anger they slew a man, and in their selfwill they digged down a wall. Cursed be their anger, for it was fierce; and their wrath, for it was cruel: I will divide them in Jacob, and scatter them in Israel.
>
> GENESIS 49:5–7 (KJV)

Your anger could be bringing a curse on you. In this Genesis passage, Jacob, at the end of his life, is ready to bless his sons, but is faced here with two of his sons who lost their blessing because of their anger. Simeon and Levi had a right to be angry. Shechem defiled their sister (Genesis 34). But they made a deal with him: If Shechem and all of his men would become circumcised, he could marry their sister. In good faith, the men of Shechem submitted to the rite of circumcision, but it was during their moment of greatest physical vulnerability and incapacity that Simeon and Levi came boldly on the city and slew all the males of Shechem.

Although they made a deal with Shechem, Simeon and Levi harbored anger in their bosom, and their anger made them vicious and vindictive. Their anger fueled their scheme and made them become tricksters, and for this Jacob cursed them. But the truth of the matter is that Jacob cursed his children with his own actions. He, too, was a schemer. He deceived his father, Isaac (Genesis 27), and his father-in-law, Laban (Genesis 30). His mother, Rebecca, was the same also. She was the one who encouraged Jacob to fool his father. Children learn from their parents and inherit their ways.

> *Choose appropriate times to discuss matters of importance.*

Anger and behavioral patters are passed down from generation to generation. If you react violently to life circumstances, your children will act the same way. Your behavior can bless or curse your children. What legacy do you want to leave? You, yourself, may act as you do because you are a child of an angry home. You must break the curse by resisting the tendency to let anger dictate your behavior. Ask God for the ability to face life with wisdom and patience. "Submit yourselves therefore to God. Resist the devil, and he will flee from you" (James 4:7, KJV). You cannot resist the curse that is in your family unless you submit to God. Don't let anger destroy your home.

Christian Anger

I'd like to take a moment to talk about a special type of anger I call Christian anger, although you can substitute any religion and the meaning is the same. I'm talking about anger that is fueled by a difference in religion. It is conflict born out of different spiritual practices and philosophies. More wars have been fought in this world over religion than any other issue. I want to make sure your home doesn't become a battlefield over faith.

Faith should strengthen your family, but often it becomes a source of contention because the faithful are zealous and the faithless are resentful. In your team, you cannot broker your religion against another team member. Your love for your family cannot be based on whether they comply with your morals as a Christian. You cannot make your children or companion accept your faith. Faith is a personal experience, and it cannot be forced. Obviously, as a Christian I want all of the people I love to be Christians and reflect my values. But the reality for many families is that there are team members who do not choose to accept Christianity, or maybe they do and choose a different denomination.

Set a guard over my mouth, O LORD: Keep watch over the door of my lips. Let not my heart be drawn To what is evil.

PSALMS 141:3–4A

(NIV)

Regardless of your religious differences, the family still must be a team. There has to be an understanding between our faith and our family. These can complement each other, but they are two distinct entities and you should remember that love between a family must be absolute. You may not condone other family members' lifestyles, but you must still love them. Your children need to know that you are committed to them regardless of what choice they make. Whether or not you endorse their practices, you are in the relationship for the long term.

Whether they are "saved" or not, you will be there. I know you want them to walk with God, but if they don't, you must still be their parents.

Countless people withhold love from their spouses, children, parents, or relatives who have otherwise been good to them, just because they do not worship the Lord the same way. In these instances, faith becomes the source of battles instead of an instrument of healing. Anger can destroy the blessings your faith should supply. You can worship, attend church regularly, and faithfully pay your tithes, but you are not blessed because your anger is a curse. It is poisoning your spirit and causing you to act in very un-Christian ways.

Reconciling family and faith is difficult when all parties involved do not share the same philosophy. Admittedly, there are times when grown children need their own place so that they can practice the life they choose without disrespecting their parents, but at no time should your love be used as leverage to force someone to believe as you do. It simply doesn't work. Be careful about throwing people off your team just because you are embarrassed by their lifestyle. They may not be godly, but they're still your parents. They may not have made the choices that you wanted them to make, but they're still your kids.

> *Don't prolong an argument just to prove you're right.*

Do not allow your faith-filled friends to coerce you into attacking your children, spouse, or parents. Some who claim to have faith may scorn your team, but people who really have faith understand family and understand the difference between the ideal that we all aspire to and the realities that many of us live with every day. Don't let outside pressure, even from your church, rip apart your team. Your church family might be well-intentioned, but who are they to judge your family? Who are they to attack your team? In the long run, in times of crisis, it's your family that is going to be there to support you.

Yes, immorality may dissolve a relationship, but immorality and faith are two separate things. There are many people who are moral but have no faith. And occasionally there are those who have faith in God but are struggling with flawed morals. It is feasible to demand that your family maintain certain moral standards, but you cannot demand that they believe what you believe. Faith is a heart issue; morality is more a line of demarcation between what is and is not acceptable behavior for your household.

Teaching your children morals is an essential part of parenting. But remember, you cannot teach people to be saved. That is an individual experience that, once you have witnessed to them, must be done through their own walk with God. Do not ransom your love, forcing them to submit to your theology before they can be a legitimate part of the family. You may want your prayers answered, your children converted, your spouse born again, but you cannot be controlling and manipulative, using your love as leverage to get what you want. Stand by your family regardless of their religious choices. Set an example they would want to follow, but don't try to drag them screaming and kicking down the path. You will only lose them completely. Let your faith be the glue that keeps your family together, not the fire that rips it apart.

Secret Anger

Although anger can be unhealthy for you and your family, it is a legitimate emotion and needs to be acknowledged. You can't keep your anger bottled up inside you, for secret anger is doubly dangerous. Secret anger takes residence in your soul and festers there like a cancer. It slowly eats away at you, replacing all your goodness with animosity and resentment. You stuff it down and keep a lid on it, but sooner or later the pressure builds up and you explode.

You never know how secret anger will eventually surface. In the mildest of circumstances, it is released as an emotional outburst, a surprise to the unsuspecting who never once glimpsed the anger so well hidden. It may simmer into a grudge, long held and bitter, infecting your relationships and undermining your family goals. It may manifest itself in vindictive schemes, manipulative maneuvers, outright deception. It can churn inside you and fuel envy, jealousy, and hatred. In its worst forms it turns violent, manifesting itself in physical or sexual abuse, or even murder.

Secret anger also harms the one who carries it. It colors your world, embittering you to all around you. As the anger percolates, you feel less joy and all your experiences are filtered through the lens of your undisclosed rage. You hate others and you hate yourself, and a pall of gray casts itself over your life. Nervous breakdowns, ulcers, and a host of physical ailments plague those who harbor anger in their bosom. Secret anger can even kill you, causing heart attacks and, some say, even cancer. Simply stated, secret anger can destroy you.

Anger can rest in the bosom of a person you think you know.

It can hide behind smiles and laughter. Anger may be simmering in the person you live with, eat with, or even sleep with. You'd be shocked by how much anger can build up in a person before it even shows. Many people are angry for years because of something seemingly insignificant their mate did early in their relationship. Twenty years and three kids later, that "insignificant" event is the foundation for their irreconcilable differences that lead them to divorce court. There are even people who harbor anger against some-

> *But it is the spirit in a man, the breath of the Almighty, that gives him understanding.*
>
> JOB 32:8 (NIV)

one who is long dead. This type of unresolved issue can stay with you for the rest of your life.

The key is communication. You need to express what you feel in a calm and acceptable manner, and your anger will dissipate. The older brother in the story of the prodigal son (Luke 15) had been angry for years, and this anger surfaced only when his father killed the fatted calf for the homecoming of his wayward younger brother. The father's reply to the older son's anger was that he was never told what the son wanted. The father's blessings were always there, and would have been freely lavished on the older son if he had communicated.

There may be no cause for your anger. Communicate and diffuse the bitter emotions that can soil your soul. Learn to manage your anger and control your emotions so that they don't control you. Unattended, they may boil over, harming you and your family and destroying any chance of your team's success.

Anger Management Is Biblical

Be ye angry, and sin not: let not the sun go down on your wrath.

EPHESIANS 4:26 (KJV)

God will never deny you the right to an emotion, but He does not want you controlled by your emotions. You have self-awareness and emotions because you were made a living soul. God does not mind your having feelings, He minds feelings having you. You have permission to be angry. In fact, Ephesians tells you it's okay to be angry. But breaking furniture, slapping your husband, or hitting your wife are not acceptable. Anytime anger causes you to damage the things God has given you charge over, your emotions are being mismanaged. Anger is not the sin; it is the mismanagement of that feeling that is the sin.

One person may rant and rave; another person may smolder and stew. Both reactions to anger are dangerous. The key is to find a way to vent anger without having an emotional explosion. The first thing to remember is that when you are angry, it means you care. You wouldn't waste your breath, your sweat, and your time to let someone know how you feel if you didn't care. You care enough to engage in conflict. What you have to do is channel that care into behavior that better serves what you care about. If you fly into a fit of rage when your child doesn't do well in school, remember that your anger has its roots in caring about your child

> *Do not allow children to become part of marital disputes.*

getting a good education and having the tools to build a productive, successful life. Does your tantrum really help your child do better in school? Sure, you can be angry at his lack of work, but instead of yelling or hitting, spend time explaining the value of education or helping him with the troubling subject. Your husband will never get saved if your mouth is constantly barking away at him. Don't hit him over the head with the Bible. Live it instead; let your management of emotions act as a role model for him.

Neither give place to the devil.

EPHESIANS 4:27 (KJV)

You give territory to the devil when you get angry. The first territory he wants to take is your house, because it is the seat of your power. He doesn't want you to have a place to rest. He wants to infiltrate your team and make it fall apart. Don't let him in. Get together in your huddle and figure out how to work things out. The issue isn't who is right or wrong; the issue isn't who is stronger or can yell louder; the issue is healing. Speak your anger to get it out of you, but speak it in love. Ask yourself and each other, "How can we work this together so that we both win?"

Let's go back to the story of Joseph to find some biblical anger-management techniques. Our friend Joseph had every reason to be angry. He had a promising future, a coat of many colors, but he was sabotaged by his brothers, stripped, and sold into slavery. He did survive, and ended up in the house of Potipher. There he was seduced by Potipher's wife and set up by her when he didn't go along with her advances. He was thrown into jail, and there he helped a fellow inmate, the butler, get out, yet the butler forgot him. Yes, Joseph had plenty of reasons to be angry. But what does he do? He doesn't get enraged, he doesn't get even. He interprets Pharaoh's dream and finds favor with him. He helps Egypt, the land that imprisoned him, survive famine. He feeds his family when they come begging for food. He forgives, and in doing so, is freed from his anger. Forgiveness is not about how the person responds to you, it is about releasing anger out of you.

Joseph had two sons. "Joseph called the name of the firstborn Manasseh: 'For God has made me forget all my toil and all my father's house' " (Genesis 41:51, NKJV). He resolved his issues of the past. He forgot everything that happened in his father's house and forgave all that caused his bad fortune. All his toil did not deter his destiny and his coming to a place of resolution of the issues in his life. Would this have happened if he had harbored

> *Forgive others and give yourself a gift, for through forgiveness you are freed from anger.*

anger in his bosom? Would he have become a powerful man in Pharaoh's command if he had gone back to Canaan to seek revenge on his brothers? No, he was able to fulfill his destiny and remain in God's favor because he controlled his emotions and resisted the temptation to get even.

Joseph had a second son, "and the name of the second he called Ephraim: 'For God has caused me to be fruitful in the land of my affliction' " (Genesis 41:52, NKJV). Joseph understood that despite all that he had endured, God blessed him anyway. You will never be completely released from your anger until you get to the point of seeing that in spite of all the ups and downs, in spite of all you have endured, you are still blessed by God. God helps you overcome, and He will help you prosper. But His blessings cannot be bestowed on you if anger gets in the way. When your emotions threaten to overwhelm you, remember that God will see you through.

Your house may seem out of control, but you can turn down the volume and tune up your family vision. You must remember that nobody is going to be everything you want him or her to be. No one is perfect. No one is "ideal." And no relationship can be truly intimate and loving and long-term without loving in spite of imperfections. Don't focus on each other's flaws, focus on your strength as a team. Put in the effort to control your emotions. Your family is worth it. How much would you give to have someone love you regardless of your status? How much would you give to have comfort come from your close connections with those you love? There can be no price placed upon the support that comes to a person whose home is intact. As I close, allow me to suggest that the suffering of the investment stage of family is nothing compared to the tremendous return you will get for years to come from those who love you.

Part Three

FAITH

10.

Faith, the Compass of My Soul

Direction is perhaps the most significant necessity for the traveler. No matter where the ultimate destination might be, the ability to determine the course is the most essential element needed for achieving the goal. If we cannot determine the direction we ought to go, then hours of travel may mean nothing at all. The effort without direction may not amount to anything of consequence. You may have movement but not progress. It is only when we have a definite course and we combine direction with movement that we obtain progress.

So where are we going? you ask. That is what all followers want to know. That is what all leaders pretend to be sure of. The reality is that most people who walk by faith have difficulty answering that one dreadful question. They have difficulty because faith is an abstract and the question is asking for a concrete answer. Faith is intangible; it can't be articulated, it can't be explained. It is something that just is.

Abraham, the patriarch of faith, demonstrates his faith when he embarks upon a journey toward a place that he has not seen and cannot describe.

And it came to pass after these things, that God did tempt Abraham, and said unto him, Abraham: and he said, Behold, here I am. And he said, Take now thy son, thine only son Isaac, whom thou lovest, and get thee into the land of Moriah; and offer him there for a burnt offering upon one of the mountains which I will tell thee of.

GENESIS 22:1–2 (KJV)

Let's look closely at the text. God directs Abraham to go the place "which I will tell thee of." Now, where in God's name is that? It is like me saying to you, "Go get in the car and start driving, and when you get where we're going I'll tell you." How frustrating that would be. But that is the way God teaches faith. He does not give details, only abstractions. So Abraham goes without knowing where he is going, but he will know when he gets there.

It reminds me of a woman shopping in a department store. Soft music plays, relaxing the shopper, trying to make her stay long enough to max out her credit cards. The woman walks through the store, looking through the racks, when from behind her she hears a soft voice: "May I help you, ma'am?"

The lady turns and smiles politely. "Well, actually I'm looking for a dress." And before she can go any further, the saleswoman is leading her to the dress department. "Here's a new design just in from Paris. It would look great on you."

The shopper tilts her head and studies the garment before shaking her head. "No, that one isn't quite right."

"Not a problem, ma'am. We have quite a large selection. How about this one?" The saleswoman smiles as she holds up another dress.

"Well, that is pretty . . . but it's not what I had in mind."

Not to be deterred, the saleswoman holds up dress after dress, but each falls short in the eyes of the customer. Finally, exasperated, the saleswoman sighs and says, "What exactly are you looking for?"

The shopper shakes her head and smiles politely. "I'm not really sure what I'm looking for, but I'll know it when I see it."

Now, that is faith. It is that thing, that place, that indescribable something that we pursue without fully being able to explain to others the unique drive we have toward it. It is that inner feeling, that "Yes, I am looking for something. There is something in here for me. I do not know exactly what it is, but when I see it, I will know it." How will I know? Quite honestly, I'm not sure. All I know is that when it is in front of me, I will know that this is it. In essence, what I'm saying is that there is a compass in our soul that informs us inwardly when it is the right dress, the right man, the right woman, or whatever it is we pursue.

Eureka!

Then on the third day Abraham lifted up his eyes, and saw the place afar off.

GENESIS 22:4 (KJV)

After three days of traveling, not really knowing where he is going, Abraham looks up and sees "the place." He sees it and immediately knows this is exactly where he is supposed to be. There is nothing more explosive than the moment we look up and see something that makes chimes ring and bells toll inside of us. It is the compass of the soul telling us, "This is the place."

If I were to continue with the example of the woman in the department store, the scenario would go something like this: The same woman who frustrated the saleswoman because she couldn't find anything she wanted now runs wildly down the aisle. She is chasing after the very same saleswoman who tried to help her before. "Tell me you have this in my size!" she breathlessly exclaims as she waves a dress in her hands. "This is it! This is exactly what I was looking for!" she shrieks excitedly. What has happened is that this woman has seen manifest on the outside what she envisioned on the inside. She couldn't explain what she was looking for—she might not even have known herself. But as soon as she sees *the* dress, she knows it is the right one. Like Abraham, she wasn't quite sure what she was looking for, she just looked until she lifted her eyes and saw "the place."

> *Jesus answered and said unto them, Verily I say unto you, If ye have faith, and doubt not, ye shall not only do this which is done to the fig tree, but also if ye shall say unto this mountain, Be thou removed, and be thou cast into the sea; it shall be done.*
>
> MATTHEW 21:21
>
> (KJV)

Now, the place is important, but the compass that guides you to it is far more important. This is the compass of the soul; this is inner direction. It is the ability to discern right from wrong. It is what enables you to know that you are on the right track and doing what you are supposed to be doing. It is Divine guidance.

Divine guidance is an invaluable resource. Without it, you are like a sailor at sea unable to find his way because he has no compass on his ship. All the waters look the same without direction. Without guidance, the sailor could spend the rest of his life moving without making any progress. I urge all of you faithful to train yourselves to listen to your inner knowledge, that instinctive certainty that tells you, "Yes, this is it!"

Visionaries See the Way

What is even more amazing is the ability to visualize something on the inside that is not manifest on the outside. When you can envision something and it becomes so real to you that you are seeing things that are not there, it is often a sign that (a) you didn't take your medication before you left the house, or (b) there is something you see inside that comes from God. It is a sign that it is out there somewhere and you have the ability to find it.

Not everyone has this ability to see the invisible. But people who do are what I call visionaries. They are guides to those who don't have it. When you see someone whose faith is so strong that they get excited about things that are not there, watch them closely. That level of passion is often an alarm going off in the spirit that what seems impossible can be done. These visionaries are the leaders of the world, men and women who can see the invisible and can do the impossible. The very fact that they can get that excited about the invisible is a sign that they can do the impossible. I am not talking about a conjured faith that comes from talking yourself into believing. I am speaking of a God-given gift of faith that enables you to see things differently from others because you have been designated to lead the way.

For example, everyone was afraid of Goliath—everyone, that is, but David. David was just a boy, but his small size had nothing to do with the magnitude of his faith. Others saw Goliath as an insurmountable problem, but David was confident that he could kill the Philistine.

> *And Saul said to David, "You are not able to go against this Philistine to fight with him: for you are a youth, and he a man of war from his youth."*
>
> *But David said to Saul, "Your servant used to keep his father's sheep, and when a lion or a bear came and took a lamb out of the flock, I went out after it and struck it, and delivered the lamb from its mouth; and when it arose against me, I caught it by its beard, and struck and killed it. Your servant has killed both lion and bear; and this uncircumcised Philistine will be like one of them, seeing he has defied the armies of the living God."*
>
> *Moreover David said, "The LORD, who delivered me from the paw of the lion and from the paw of the bear, He will deliver me from the hand of this Philistine."*
>
> 1 SAMUEL 17:33–37 (NKJV)

David had faith in himself and in God. He knew, in no uncertain terms, that God would give him the ability to slay Goliath. That kind of faith is Divine ennoblement. At a complete disadvantage—because of his smaller size and his substandard equipment—David was still able to achieve what he was able to believe. David was the only man who could defeat Goliath because he was the only one who had the faith for it. He knew this was the place, a destiny place.

This was for him a life-changing, pivotal point. Had he missed this opportunity, he would have spent his life in the field, tending sheep. But he knew what he had to do. His compass was screaming like a fire alarm. He didn't fully know why himself. It was not just the defeating of Goliath that was at stake. Goliath was just a marker on the road of his life, and there was an inner voice saying—no, screaming—"Turn here!"

This is not the kind of faith that can be conferred or conjured. It cannot be achieved by focusing on a thought all day and using mind power. You either have it or you do not. Don't try to eat when you are not hungry or fight when you are not angered. Don't try to adopt something that isn't given to you. The problem with some people is that they keep trying to fight someone else's giant. You have the power only when you have the vision for the task. There is nothing as frustrating as being stuck with a task for which you have no conviction. You'll never succeed. But when you have a conviction, you can do anything!

I could give you countless biblical examples—like Gideon, who single-handedly defeated the Midianites (Judges 6–8); Queen Esther, who risked her life to save the Jews of Shushan (Esther); and Noah (Genesis 6–9). Can you imagine how crazy everyone thought Noah was? He built a giant ark and filled it with animals. His neighbors must have thought him a madman, trying to build a floating zoo! But Noah knew what he had to do. He listened to the voice of God, and when the flood came, he and his family were safe. He followed his inner compass, and he and his family were blessed.

I could step back into history and introduce you to visionaries like Benjamin Franklin, who flew his kite in a rainstorm. Or Anne Sullivan, who was Helen Keller's teacher. No one could do anything with this belligerent, angry child whose blindness and deafness had left her confused and disturbed. But Ms. Sullivan had the vision for the task. More recently there was Martin Luther King, Jr., who fought for civil rights, and Nelson Mandela, who defied apartheid in South Africa.

> *Faith sees the invisible, believes the unbelievable, and receives the impossible.*
> CORRIE TEN BOOM

These men and women defied the odds and achieved greatness. They had a vision and they followed it, despite the doubts of others and obstacles that were in their way. They persevered by faith. They were remarkable, one of a kind. They weren't gods; they weren't perfect. They were just compass-carrying men and women who were able to see the invisible and therefore do the impossible. The question you must ask yourself is "What can I see that others cannot?" Whatever the answer is, that is what you have the power to perform.

Faith, the Hallucinogen

Enough of my ranting about these ghosts of faith whose testimonies seem far removed from contemporary or normal challenges. Allow me the privilege of telling you about an experience that I had as a young preacher in a small, backwoods town called

Smithers near a coal camp in West Virginia. I was in my mid-twenties, and I had been pastoring near there in a place called Montgomery, also a small town. One day, I was taking one of the parishioners home, and we passed a building I had never seen before. "Wow," I thought to myself, "what a great place! It would make a wonderful church!" I thought the building was so beautiful that I literally stopped the car in the middle of the road. I was so excited that I leapt out of the car and tried to peek into the building to see what was inside.

Now, had you been the parishioner in the car with me, you would have thought I had lost my mind. You see, the building was a condemned old movie theater that hadn't been occupied in several decades. The roof was torn off in major sections. Plants were growing on the inside, the doors were leaning, and the place stunk to high heaven. On top of that, there were rats the size of a size-nine shoe scampering all over the place. But I didn't really notice any of that. I thought the building was perfect. The first time I went into the building, I fell through the floor to my shoulders as I was walking up the steps. With most of my body beneath floor level and my brother trying to pull me out, I was looking up at the building talking about where I was going to place the choir!

I will never forget the first time I brought our little congregation over to see this miracle of a building. I was shocked when we opened the door and they looked totally disgusted. I couldn't understand why they weren't excited. One of the congregation literally threw up and had to leave because the smell was so bad. I wondered what was wrong with her, but I kept walking through, shining my flashlight and telling them how nice the building would be when I finished repairing it.

You see, people who are visionaries see things that are not there. If you have been seeing things that are not there, it could be that you are not hallucinating but are a person pregnant with a miracle and about to do the impossible. One of the signs of a Divine intervention in your life is when you can see clearly what others cannot see. Your faith is the greatest evidence imaginable that you can achieve what you can conceive!

> *But as it is written, Eye hath not seen, nor ear heard, neither have entered into the heart of man, the things which God hath prepared for them that love him.*
>
> *But God hath revealed them unto us by his Spirit: for the Spirit searcheth all things, yea, the deep things of God.*
>
> *For what man knoweth the things of a man, save the spirit of man which is in him? Even so the things of God knoweth no man, but the Spirit of God.*
>
> *Now we have received, not the spirit of the world, but the spirit which is of God; that we might know the things that are freely given to us of God.*
>
> 1 CORINTHIANS 2:9–12 (KJV)

I don't speak of this mighty faith to elicit admiration for the people who have it; I want you to gain an understanding of the God who gave it. This is not self-induced faith. It is divinely a result of a conviction in your spirit that supersedes your senses and defies what your eyes have or have not seen. Whenever you are able to have this death-defying, odds-ignoring, tenacious conviction, it is indicative that you will achieve great things. It is God's way of revealing His plan for you.

I Submit Exhibit A

Now faith is the substance of things hoped for, the evidence of things not seen.

HEBREWS 11:1 (KJV)

The Scripture says that faith is evidence of things unseen. In other words, faith proves that what is conceived and not yet manifest will actually come to fruition. It is the spiritual exhibition of things unseen. It is admissible as proof of the promised possession. Now, let me be clear about this. It is not *obtaining* what I believe that proves it is possible. The fact that I have this relentless, hell-bent conviction about something that others do not see is evidence enough that it is possible. My absolute faith is God telling me that what I conceive I can achieve.

Now, many years have passed since I saw that building in Smithers for the first time. We did buy it and convert it into a church. It is still functioning as a church today. I have been gone from Smithers for years, but the church still stands as proof of my convictions, proof that what I envisioned internally could be made into reality. The church is proof to the world, but my faith was evidence enough for me. My faith was so strong that I knew the decrepit building I was seeing could be a glorious church. It is only in retrospect that I realize how ridiculous I must have looked with my arms flailing and my body falling through the floor—still smiling and planning and seeing the invisible.

I will not say opening that church was easy. By the time I had gotten the loan, which was not nearly enough for the work that needed to be done, and had opened the building for service, my lights were off at home and my feet were bleeding from long and abusive hours of physical sacrifice. But we did it. I can still see the tears of joy on my wife's face when I cut the ribbon to dedicate that little church on the side of the road. It was a glamorous auditorium to us, because we knew whence it had come.

> *Even when your faith in God wavers, God's faith in you remains firm. Therefore being justified by faith, we have peace with God through our Lord Jesus Christ.*
> ROMANS 5:1 (KJV)

Years later, when my work was finished there and I had moved to the next church, someone asked me, "How could you work that hard for something and then leave it?" The answer is a bit complicated. First of all, one can only make the impossible possible when one has a burning conviction. When that is gone, the first thing you should try to do is get some rest and ascertain whether it is temporary burnout or not. If, after you have thoroughly rested, you still have lost your passion for that work, you might do well to pass the baton to someone who has the grace to take the dream to the next level. I was standing in the way of the next pastor's giant! I had killed mine, and it was time for the next one.

Another issue is even more significant than the first. It is not the things that God gives you that mean the most to you. It is the things you learn about Him and about yourself that have the lasting effect. I left the building there in Smithers, but I took my faith with me. The faith that I took with me had been strengthened in

154

that experience, and I had new hope and a fresh dream. Often, the best thing that comes out of the conquest is not the victory achieved but the lessons learned. Having learned my lessons at Smithers, I was ready to graduate and move on, taking my knowledge and faith with me and building upon them along the way.

The Essential Equation

For it is with your heart that you believe and are justified, and it is with your mouth that you confess and are saved.

ROMANS 10:10 (NIV)

Let's take a look at this simple yet profound statement. It encapsulates the whole idea of Christian conversion. First, it teaches that you believe with your heart. This is faith. This is knowing in your heart, having the conviction that you can achieve what you are after. It goes on to say that faith constitutes justification, for you wouldn't have that kind of absolute conviction if your endeavor weren't sanctioned by God. Then it says that it is with the mouth that you confess. Here we have the power of confession. Finally, the sentence crescendos with the ultimate experience: "and are saved." This is the ultimate goal in the text. The goal is salvation.

But the process should not be left here as if it were simply the cocoon from which the beautiful butterfly of salvation has emerged. No, this may be the catalyst of the new birth, but it is too valuable to be limited to that one-time experience. The principle taught here is one that you should take to heart. I want you to walk away from Romans 10:10 knowing the simple equation that applies to all of life:

$$Conviction + Confession = Change$$

When you have a belief planted firmly in your heart and you speak that belief, you will effect change. It adds up only when both elements are present. Conviction without confession is like faith without works: It is dead. Confession without conviction is the noisy boasting of a loud mouth and an empty head. But if the mouth confesses what the heart is convinced of, it produces a strong elixir that will bring about change. It changed the country when Dr. Martin Luther King, Jr., opened his mouth and spoke what his heart believed. It changed how the world viewed civil liberties. Dr. King combined convictions with confession and he changed the world.

Conviction + Confession = Change. If the mouth speaks what the heart believes, mountains can be moved, giants can be killed, nations can be conquered, laws can be changed, and on and on and on.

Follow the Faithful

Faith. Who needs it? Everyone needs it. It is not restricted to church houses, synagogues, or temples. It is not contained in stained glass, prayer beads, or icons. It transcends baptisms and burials, rituals and routines. It is more than rhetoric; it is reality. It is more than creeds and crosses; it is strong, hard, relentless, reckless, unsinkable determination to bring about a change. It is in the hearts of men and women who are called to be the mothers of invisible dreams and the fathers of causes unbelievable to other people. Whenever you see real, raw, unpretentious faith in anybody, watch them. They are giant killers, mountain movers, and life changers. They know the equation. These are the people who will lead the way into the twenty-first century. Their eyes are on fire, and they can take less and do more with it because they have been empowered by that thing called faith to go to that "place" they have not been.

> *Remember those who rule over you, who have spoken the word of God to you, whose faith follow, considering the outcome of their conduct.*
>
> HEBREWS 13:7 (NKJV)

These are the leaders whom we must follow. Not because they are great people, but because they are ordinary people with great faith. They, through the Spirit of God, have been designated drivers, meant to usher us into new places and beyond the walls of Jericho into the land of milk and honey. Their faith is a sign that we can go beyond where we are and take control of giants that are too big for us.

When you see a radical person who scales walls and climbs mountains, for God sake, don't try to tame them. Follow them! Their faith is the conviction needed to constitute a change. These are the Sons of Thunder. When you see them, choose them as leaders, for they are leaders and they will lead.

If you want to be successful, follow them. Imitate their faith. Adopt it. You cannot duplicate it, but you can imitate it in your life, in your challenges. You can use the principles of faith. Wherever you have the conviction, make the confession, and when you do, expect a change!

11.

Without a Touch

The other disciples therefore said unto him, We have seen the LORD. But he said unto them, Except I shall see in his hands the print of the nails, and put my finger into the print of the nails, and thrust my hand into his side, I will not believe.

And after eight days again his disciples were within, and Thomas with them: then came Jesus, the doors being shut, and stood in the midst, and said, Peace be unto you.

Then saith he to Thomas, Reach hither thy finger, and behold my hands; and reach hither thy hand, and thrust it into my side: and be not faithless, but believing.

And Thomas answered and said unto him, My LORD and my God. Jesus saith unto him, Thomas, because thou hast seen me, thou hast believed: blessed are they that have not seen, and yet have believed.

JOHN 20:25–29 (KJV)

Thomas needed to see Jesus with his own eyes and touch His wounds with his own hands before he could believe the Christ had been resurrected. He needed rock-solid, no-room-for-doubt proof that Jesus had risen from the dead. Although he had been a loyal follower of the Son of God, when the other apostles told him the promise had been fulfilled and Jesus had risen, he simply could not believe by faith alone.

Now, before we become too critical of Thomas's weakened theology, remember that he had been an eyewitness to the death of Christ. There is nothing as convincing as being present when someone expires. Imagine seeing the last breath gush from His bleeding lips. Thomas saw Christ's naked body writhe one final time in total agony; he saw His eyes roll back into His skull; he saw Him "give up the ghost." Thomas saw His stiff body removed from the cross; he saw the congealed blood on His wounds. Thomas saw with his own eyes the degrading death of Jesus, and there was no doubt in his mind that He was dead. Everything his experience had taught him, his eyes had shown him, confirmed that He was invariably dead—d-e-a-d, dead!

> Men can be attracted but not forced to the faith. You may drive people to baptism, but you won't move them one step further in religion.
>
> ALCUIN

What a shock, what an embarrassment, that their Hero had demonstrated His humanity by dying publicly, naked on the cross. They had called him Lord, but He died like a common criminal. There were no chariots of fire, as there were for Elijah. There was no whirlwind, no lightning. Just an agonizing death that suggested that Jesus was just a man.

Having witnessed this spectacle, the disciples experienced a full range of emotions. Some stared in disbelief, some walked down the road to Emmaus, some started swearing, and some started doubting. Still others locked themselves up, either out of shame or out of fear of being killed for having been apart of such a "ridiculous idea" in the first place.

As if their Lord's death isn't confusing enough, then someone says that He is alive again. But Thomas is unwilling to be confused again. He has already quit his job, left his family, committed his life to a man who died like a thief on the cross. Seeing his Lord crucified makes Thomas question his faith, so he makes up his mind to trust only what he can perceive through his senses. That is generally what we do when faith seems to fail. We cleave to the practical, the absolute, the tangible. We discard faith as if it were an old coat ready for the trash and drape ourselves in the sound truth of what we can touch, what we "know" to be absolute.

Thomas can't believe by faith anymore, so he makes a bold declaration that wins him the nickname "Doubting Thomas." He says, "Unless I feel the nail prints in His hand and touch the piercing in His side, I will not believe." In other words, none of this faith business for me.

Philosophies of Faith

Thomas does get the physical evidence he needs, and ultimately, when all is said and done, the end is faith. He enters into faith based on what he saw and touched. But Jesus says to him, "You have believed because you have seen. But blessed are they who have not seen and yet they believe." Jesus acknowledges that Thomas has faith again, but he applauds those who have faith without physical evidence.

As long as he believes, what difference does it make? I'm glad you asked. Suppose Thomas, like millions of other people, was not afforded the opportunity to touch and see. Would that failed opportunity alter the facts of the resurrection? Of course not! Jesus was alive whether Thomas got to see Him or not.

> For what if some did not believe? Will their unbelief make the faithfulness of God without effect? Certainly not! Indeed, let God be true but every man a liar. . . .
>
> ROMANS 3:3–4 (NKJV)

The luxury of seeing first before you believe may limit you from receiving many things that God wants you to embrace simply because He said so. Thomas ultimately believes, and he became an adamant witness until he was martyred. He was faithfully committed, but not because he had developed the kind of relationship with Christ that established trust. He believed because he was depending on his senses more than his relationships. Had Thomas not gotten to spend those few minutes with Jesus, he would have been lost, robbed of the greatest gift possible. Lost because he had limited himself to one method of believing: He believed only with his senses. But you and I know that senses are not always that accurate.

Criminal justice experts tell us that the most unreliable evidence is an eyewitness. Yet it sounds so damning to say to the alleged criminal, "We have an eyewitness who saw you at the scene of the crime." It sounds damning because we have so much confidence in our senses. But case after case will show you that people seldom know what they saw. Eyes play tricks and deceive. It's what magicians base their entire act on. Do you think he really saws the lady in half? Does the table float in midair? It is sleight of hand, optical illusions, and we believe what we see, but it is not real.

Don't Touch

On the Sunday after Jesus' crucifixion, just three days after His death, Mary Magdalene goes to His tomb. When she gets there, she is horrified to see the stone has been taken away from the opening and the tomb is empty. She is distraught, but soon her distress is replaced by surprise. For standing before her is Jesus, raised from the dead.

> *Jesus saith unto her, Touch me not; for I am not yet ascended to my Father: but go to my brethren, and say unto them, I ascend unto my Father, and your Father; and to my God, and your God.*
>
> JOHN 20:17 (KJV)

He tells Mary Magdalene, one of His greatest admirers, not to touch Him. He stands before her; she heard his voice and sought to touch Him. Yet He does not allow that touch. This was a woman who washed His feet with her tears, and now she can't touch Him. A touch would have been a way to affirm what her ears had heard and her eyes had seen. But Jesus doesn't indulge her the luxury of touching Him. He allows her to witness His word but not His flesh. She would have to go back and tell the others He had risen, but she would be a witness who testified without a touch.

Many would later say that they handled the body of the Lord. They would say that they saw Him eat fish or that they touched Him after He rose from the dead. But Mary would be able to say, "I accepted Him without a touch."

This story is significant because many times we, too, are required to bypass our senses and embrace our conviction. We must believe without the crutch of sensual perception. Without a tutor to teach us for three years, without witnessing the raising of the dead or the walking on water, we must believe. As we pursue our quest in the Kingdom and in the world in which we live, we will be required to believe, without the benefit of our senses, against all odds, that we will achieve whatever we set out to do.

Sensual Faith

So much of what we believe is based on what we can receive through our senses. Our senses give us the ability to decipher everything around us. The tangible becomes the point of reference for most of our thinking. It is through our senses that we receive and understand instructions. We depend on our senses to inform us and lead us through this world.

But Hebrews 11 is devoted to telling us what the early patriarchs did by faith. It discusses Abel, Enoch, and Noah. It recounts the achievements of Abraham, Sarah, Jacob, Joseph, and Moses. It goes on and on, talking about the great men and women of the Bible and what they accomplished because of their faith—not their senses, but their faith.

Now faith is the substance of things hoped for, the evidence of things not seen. For by it the elders obtained a good testimony.

HEBREWS 11:1–2 (NKJV)

You see, the elders were blessed because they had a faith so strong that they clung to it, sometimes in opposition to their senses. Had David just used his senses, he would have gone running when he saw the giant Goliath. Goliath was so much bigger and stronger, and David was just a boy. But David's faith that God would give him the power to overcome the Philistine was so strong that he was able to do it. The Bible is full of stories of those whose faith enabled them to perform superhuman feats, feats they would never have thought possible if they had to determine the outcome by their senses alone.

And what more shall I say? For the time would fail me to tell of Gideon and Barak and Samson and Jephthah, also of David and Samuel and the prophets: who through faith subdued kingdoms, worked righteousness, obtained promises, stopped the mouths of lions, quenched the violence of fire, escaped the edge of the sword, out of weakness were made strong, became valiant in battle, turned to flight the armies of the aliens. Women received their dead raised to life again.

HEBREWS 11:32–35 (NKJV)

165

There are times when faith makes no sense. How can a sea be parted? How can one man defeat an entire army? How can the entire world have been created by the word of God? It is having to believe in spite of our senses that makes some so-called intellectuals say that faith is for the simple-minded, the gullible, the easily fooled. But under closer scrutiny, we find that even the most intellectually astute and practical minded have to function on some level of faith.

How can we avoid faith? The investor who puts money in the stock market does it by faith. No one knows from day to day which way the stocks will go, yet millions of dollars are spent every day in the stock market—something that has absolutely no guarantees. The person who makes a career move after years of being with one company has no guarantee the new job will work out. The new company doesn't know either, so they put the employee on a ninety-day probation. Yet he moves his children across the country, buys a house, and starts a new life. He does it by faith. We can even apply this to the most mundane of situations. A tired mother stops by a fast-food restaurant and orders six burgers, three soft drinks, and a large fries. She drives to the window and gives her money to an absolute stranger without checking the contents of the bag. She drives away confident that she got what she paid for. That's faith. It's virtually impossible to go twenty-four hours and not do anything that demands some element of faith.

> *Faith is believing in things when common sense tells you not to.*
> GEORGE SEATON

Faith is the unavoidable by-product of uncertainty. We have

to develop some degree of faith to endure the many questions for which life provides no answers. The longer you live, the more you realize that so much in life is uncertain. Why, you don't even know if you will live to see tomorrow.

Some of you may be thinking that of course there are some concrete truths. Scientific facts can be proven in laboratory tests. Scientific facts? Like the fact that the earth is flat? Like the fact that the sun revolves around the earth? Both examples were considered concrete truths until more advanced technology proved them incorrect. More research, better equipment, and before you know it "facts" become fiction. What is scientific fact today may be absolute folly tomorrow.

And how many of us really understand all that science, anyway? Every day thousands of us board 747s that fly us all over the world. Someone could explain the physics, but would the average person be able to grasp it? So when all is said and done, we are thirty thousand feet in the air totally by faith! Even if we comprehend the mechanics of flying, we still have no guarantee that something won't go wrong, that there won't be some kind of malfunction. It's all about faith.

Ultimately, at some time or another every day, each of us is required to operate based on faith—whether that is faith in God, faith in what we read, or faith in what someone promised. You cannot function without faith. How would you let your children leave the house if you didn't have faith that they would come home safe? How would you get into a car and drive if you didn't have faith that the other motorists would obey the rules of the road? With no proof and little awareness, we all practice faith every day.

No Christian—or Buddhist, Muslim, or Jew, for that matter—should ever be embarrassed by their faith, because everyone operates in some area of faith. It's just that we have our faith in God. I am unapologetically Christian. I believe in Jesus Christ. There are people who disagree with my convictions, but that is all right. I know in Whom I believe. And although I haven't seen Him, I have faith in Him.

Tap into the Power of God

And Jesus answering saith unto them, Have faith in God.

MARK 11:22 (KJV)

In this verse, Jesus is telling us to have confidence in the sovereign ability of God to judiciously rule over His creation, making decisions that are best for the overall good of mankind. "Have faith in God" is a commandment that relieves us of the urge to put our faith in people, places, or things; it takes our faith from the unreliable and puts it into the Divine, which is ever faithful, dependent, and sure. "Have faith in God" relieves us of the stress of always having to have an answer to every question, an antidote for every problem, and a cure for every crisis. When we can't see tomorrow, we can trust the One Who can to make the right turns now to get us where we need to go. When we can't trust ourselves, we can depend on His more excellent wisdom to know what's best for us.

Thomas's problem was not a lack of faith; it was misdirected faith. He had faith in the physical, tangible things he could access with his own human attributes. But Jesus is teaching a deeper level of faith. He is teaching us to have faith in God, Whose ability transcends our own limited resources. Have faith in God and tap into the power.

Blessed are those who have not seen and yet they believe. Blessed are those whose faith has moved beyond the tangible and the natural into the supernatural. Yet there are many who call themselves Christians, but when you get to the fine print remain doubtful. For instance, I have had believers ask me questions like How did you get this or that? When I tell them the Lord just worked it out, they almost scoff, seemingly saying, "Yeah, yeah, but really, what did you do?" Obviously, these people do not believe that God, and God alone, is sovereign enough to just bless you.

> *Faith is the first factor in a life devoted to service. Without it, nothing is possible. With it, nothing is impossible.*
>
> MARY MCLEOD BETHUNE

When God gets ready to bless you, He just does. He does it because He can. He does it because it pleases Him to do so. He does it because it fits into some greater purpose. People who do not have fully developed faith in God try to sneak around like Delilah, trying to find out the secret of your strength.

> *Then she said to him, "How can you say, 'I love you,' when your heart is not with me? You have mocked me three times, and have not told me where your great strength lies." And it came to pass, when she pestered him daily with her words and pressed him, so that his soul was vexed to death, that he told her all his heart, and*

said to her, "No razor has ever come upon my head, for I have been a Nazirite to God from my mother's womb. If I am shaven, then my strength will leave me, and I shall become weak, and be like any other man."

When Delilah saw that he had told her all his heart, she went and called for the lords of the Philistines, saying, "Come up once more, for he has told me all his heart." So the lords of the Philistines came up to her and brought the money in their hand. Then she lulled him to sleep on her knees, and called for a man and had him shave off the seven locks of his head. Then she began to torment him, and his strength left him.

JUDGES 16:15–19 (NKJV)

Delilah questions Samson's strength because he doesn't look that strong. She knows he is receiving his strength from some other source, and she wants to know his secret. In truth, Samson's strength isn't in his arms, but it isn't in his hair, either. His strength is in his heart. His secret is his faith in God. His covenant is safe until he discloses that his faith in God necessitates that he not give his heart to anyone else. But Samson gives Delilah "all his heart." Bad mistake! Once he does that, she knows his secret. She cuts his hair, which is an outer sign of his faith in God in his heart. Samson transfers his faith from God and deposits it in Delilah, someone he shouldn't have faith in, someone he shouldn't trust. He removes his faith in God and puts his faith in Delilah, and as a result he loses his strength.

The Formula of Faith

God has dealt to every man a measure of faith. Yet some people seem to have far more faith than others. That is because faith is like a muscle and must be exercised. It's like a newborn baby who is so weak that he cannot hold his own head up. It is not that he doesn't have the muscles required to do this. It's just that those muscles are not yet developed. Similarly, your faith needs to be developed.

The best way to exercise a weak muscle is to expose it to resistance. Trials and tribulations are the training tools of faith. When you face a difficult time and God brings you through it, you develop faith that He will bring you through the next crisis. The more resistance training, the stronger the muscle of faith.

A personal trainer will tell you that repetitions bring results. When it comes to building muscles, how much weight you carry is not as important as how many repetitions you do. The more reps, the more you will be strengthened, and the more weight you will eventually be able to bear. If you lift five pounds over and over again, eventually you will master the five-pound curl and can move on to ten pounds. So it is with responsibility and growth in the spirit. If you can master faith on one level, you can master it on another. You begin to understand that if God brought you through that, He can bring you through this.

> *For we walk by faith, not by sight.*
> 2 CORINTHIANS 5:7
> (KJV)

We need to faith-train. That's why I believe it is crucial to go through the process and experience both success and failure. It's

important to stretch the muscle of your faith. I thank God that I
went through many of the things I have. It all has prepared me. It
has strengthened me and equipped me. If you look back over
your life, I'm sure you will recall challenges you faced. But I'm
sure you will also see that those challenges prepared you for
future endeavors.

This is how David destroyed Goliath. He learned the formula
through past experiences. He faced the lion and the bear, but
these experiences were just training for his encounter with the
Philistine. His experiences were his training, they were his tests.
He passed those tests, and now he has the skill to pass this test
with Goliath. David knows the power of experience, and for this
reason refuses Saul's armor because he has not "tested" it.

> Moreover David said, "The LORD, who delivered me from the
> paw of the lion and from the paw of the bear, He will deliver me
> from the hand of this Philistine."
> And Saul said to David, "Go, and the LORD be with you!"
> So Saul clothed David with his armor, and he put a bronze
> helmet on his head; he also clothed him with a coat of mail.
> David fastened his sword to his armor and tried to walk, for he
> had not tested them. And David said to Saul, "I cannot walk
> with these, for I have not tested them." So David took them off.
>
> 1 SAMUEL 17:37–39 (NKJV)

You can use only what you have proved. This is important to
know in this business of faith. You can't use someone else's workout
for your Goliath. I remember listening to one of my church members, Deion Sanders, talk about how he trains for football. Deion

was often critiqued because he didn't train with the rest of his team. He said to me one day, "They want me to work out with them, but what they do doesn't work for me. I have my own way of training, but when I go on the field I will be ready to play with my team."

You may not train the way others do, but as long as you get the form down pat, you can get the results. David would not use what Saul had trained with because he had not proven it. The things you are facing now may be your lion or bear. They may have been sent to prepare you. They may have been sent so you can work on your formula.

Have you ever noticed that people who are millionaires can lose everything, go bankrupt, and two years later be back on top? You know why? They know the formula. They may have lost everything, but they still have the formula. The formula is better than the riches. If you get the formula, it will work anywhere. If you can cook, you can cook anywhere. If you can sing, you can sing anywhere. Learn God's formula for your life. Learn the formula that gets results in your life.

Get Ready for the Big Time

. . . Well done, thou good and faithful servant: thou has been faithful over a few things, I will make thee ruler over many things: enter thou into the joy of thy lord.

MATTHEW 25:21 (KJV)

Once you master the formula on a small scale, you are ready for a promotion. "Have faith in God" is the formula. Once you master not having faith in your limited talent, other people's promises, whom you know, and so on, you are ready to move on to the big league. God will make you ruler over many things once you master smaller things. But you need to master the form.

I have seen people go from one bad marriage right into another. They never stop to find out what is wrong with the form. It might be the kind of people they select. It might be how tightly they cling to them. It might me that they give too much too quickly. I don't know. But I do know that if the form isn't repaired, the results won't change. Bad form with five-pound weights will be bad form with ten-pound weights. You cannot move up if you don't have the form perfected.

What is most important as you work on your form is that you understand the message that was taught to old Doubting Thomas. Sometimes it is more blessed to believe without a touch than to have proof to believe. In spite of the obstacles that are against you, you can still prevail if you have faith in God. You don't have to have a dime in your pocket, a friend on the phone, a contact in high places, or anything else before God moves on your behalf. What you do have to have in order to be successful is simple:

1. Possess it by faith: Know in your heart that it is meant to be yours.
2. Work out your faith: Have the tenacity to go through the trials and tribulations before you attempt to conquer what you haven't trained for.

3. Natural resistance requires Divine assistance: To avoid the mistake of trusting undependable people, promises, or statistics, count only on God.

4. Don't lose your form as you add more weight: Maintain your faith no matter what you face.

5. Today's fight is training for an easier tomorrow: Persevere through your trials, for they are training you for greater things. They help you perfect your form.

If you can remember these five things, your faith will take you to places you've never been, show you things you've never seen, and perform miracles in your life beyond your wildest dreams. No matter what your enemies say, no matter what your senses say, trust that God will perform mightily for you. You can bank on it . . . without a touch!

12.

Faith Develops in the Dark!

H ave you ever thought about the process that is involved in photography? From the point that you get your family posed with smiles on their faces to the final framed photo, you have to go through a number of steps. When you take a photo, you expose the film in your camera to light by opening the shutter. The light reacts with something called silver-halide particles in the film. These light-sensitive particles react to the light, producing an invisible reaction. The film must be developed in order for the reaction to be made visible. To keep the film from getting overexposed, the film is developed in a dark, cool room using several chemicals. The skill of the photographer comes into play, because he must know how long to keep the film in each chemical. An error in the process and the photo could come out too dark, too light, streaked, or stained. But it is only after each step is performed for the right duration of time that you end up with a perfect picture.

The development of our faith is similar to that of film development. We are exposed to the light of life, but the image of the Master is not seen until we endure the processes of life. It is in the dark that our lives are dipped into the developers that expose who and what we are. The Master knows how long to keep us in each chemical bath; He knows how much we can handle, and He leaves us in the bath only until we develop into the desired image. He moves us from one experience to another, and although we do not see the full, final image until the process is complete, we can trust that the process that takes place in the dark will eventually produce a clear image.

What Is Faith?

Faith is a living, breathing organism. It is so full of vitality that it exudes the strength that causes tombstones to roll back, Red Seas to part, and mountains to slide into the sea. The business of faith can be at once both an electrifying and a gut-wrenching, life-altering power. Faith is what enables us to deal with the temporal and look forward to the eternal. Faith allows us to believe in the sweet promise of the hereafter encased in the bitter here and now. It is by faith that we live righteously today so that we might live again tomorrow. In faith, the strong-willed person has the tenacity and trust in God's promise to keep moving toward a dream and thereby achieve it.

Faith is all of the above, but it transcends these limited definitions. In truth, faith has the elasticity to daily redefine itself based on the things that are hoped for. So, depending on what is hoped for, that is the ingredient your faith becomes. If in the wilderness with Israel there was a hope of bread, faith became the flour and the eggs of it. If there was a thirst, faith was the water that sprang out of a rock. If there was sickness, it became the medicinal influence that healed those infected with plagues and disease.

Faith is many things; faith is everything. But despite all of its ambiguities, faith is always miraculous. Faith gave Abel's blood the ability of speech; it turned Moses' rod into a slithering, murdering serpent. Faith turned dust to boils and fought back the witches of Egypt. Faith, my friend, is what caused David to survive the javelins of Saul and collect the foreskins of his enemies. It made him soft enough to sing poetry and strong enough to cut through the bloody neck of his opponent. Though David had come only to bring a lunch to his hungry brothers in the field, by his faith he left not only with lunch but also with the severed head of the enemy of Israel.

> *Faith is like radar that sees through the fog— the reality of things at a distance that the human eye cannot see.*
>
> CORRIE TEN BOOM

Faith is a force to be reckoned with. It resists terminal cancer, scoffs at statistics, defies doctors, ignores X rays, and stands up to judicial systems undaunted and unafraid. Faith is the currency of heaven itself.

Faith is what made Winnie Mandela refuse to move out of her house even though it was riddled with bullet holes by men shooting in the night. Faith is what made Dr. Janusz Korczak, the Jewish teacher in Poland, establish a school for children in the ghetto. When the school was closed by the Nazi regime, he dressed his children in their best clothes and made the journey with them to their ultimate deaths in the concentration camp. With their heads held high, they refused to succumb to the degrading debauchery around them. Faith is what enabled Joan of Arc to pray while the stench of her burning flesh filled her nostrils. Faith is the ingredient that enabled Medgar Evers's wife, Myrlie Evers, to refuse to rest until the injustice of her husband's murder was vindicated in the indictment of the savage criminals who killed him. Faith is what took Colonel Harlan Sanders from living off a $105-a-month Social Security check to running a $285-billion company, working with only a piece of chicken and twenty-nine different spices tossed in a bag with flour! All of these heroes passed through the darkroom in order to develop themselves. All of them seemed somehow empowered by an inner strength in a dark place. I bet many of them would have preferred an easier road to greatness. They would have liked to avoid the dark and painful developmental stages. But our silver halides of faith that cause us to shine come only when we are processed through and by the darkrooms of life.

Faith to Die For

When I write to you about faith, I want to go beyond the polished, camera-ready faith that ends up in the Hall of Fame. I don't want to discuss faith that brings a hundredfold return without warning you that a harvest is the end result of a death. Walking through the valley of the shadow of death is what causes goodness and mercy to develop in our lives. This will not be accomplished in a one-hour drive-by experience with life. It will require a process and a Developer who knows how to cause His image to be reflected through the dark shadows of life.

As I write this, I am preparing to eulogize a young man who grew up with my children. They were raised in the same Sunday school class. Jason, like so many other little boys, was playful and rambunctious as he climbed and squirmed all over the little chairs at church. It is hard to think that the little boy we all knew and loved was—after a twenty-four-hour search—dragged out of the bottom of the river and is now lying in a morgue on a slab. He was just eighteen years old.

His parents, newly appointed pastors, now lead the West Virginia congregation I have long since left. I struggle as I try to write the eulogy. What do you say to people who believe in miracles when one doesn't happen? What do you say when we read all of those glossy stories of supernatural spectacular miracles and then, when we so needed one, one did not occur?

> *Let us hold fast the profession of our faith without wavering; for he is faithful that promised.*
>
> HEBREWS 10:23
>
> (KJV)

Well, I will go to the funeral and try to help in any way that I can. I will try to bring comfort and ease the anguish that even the most faithful feel when life has no reason or rhyme. If it weren't for the message I have gleaned from observing the seeds I saw my mother store in the kitchen, I would be at a loss for words.

The seeds were hard and dry, kept in the dark and left untouched until planting time. It was when they were placed in the ground and the outer encasement died that the inner life came flooding out. The death of the seed is the life of the plant.

Jason, like most of us, had a hard time getting his real self to come out. The outer encasement often blocks the real life of the inner self from emerging. But like the seed, the cessation of the outside life doesn't necessarily mean the end of the inside life. The inside life of the soul lies trapped under the deep layers of our outer self, and sometimes only God can get it out of us.

In truth, it is not only Jason who is planted like a seed. Through his tragic loss, new life and answers emerge, friends and family reevaluate life itself, and those who were once far off draw near again. Even his parents, agonizing in what is every parent's nightmare, will emerge from the darkness with a faith that is unsinkable. Yes, it aches and the darkness is frightening, but when all is said and done, they may well find some unknown or formerly undefined image left on their soul.

> *All these died in faith, without receiving the promises, but having seen them and having welcomed them from a distance, and having confessed that they were strangers and exiles on the earth. For those who say such things make it clear that they are seeking a country of their own. And indeed if they had been thinking of that country from which they went out, they would have had opportunity to return. But as it is, they desire a better country, that is, a heavenly one. Therefore God is not ashamed to be called their God.*
>
> HEBREWS 11:13–16 (NASB)

I started writing this chapter before Jason's death occurred, lest you think I am practicing my sermon on you. The reality is that wisdom is the eulogy of life's painful experiences. I speak of Jason not only because my heart is full of him and his life will leave an indelible mark on all of those who loved him; I use him to illustrate to you that faith is not always glowing and easily obtained. It is often the result of agony so intense that the spirit trembles, the will breaks, the eyes leak. Only much later does the soul profit from the experience. Jason is only a metaphor I use to underscore that dreams are often slammed against the wall of unexpected adversity. The company loses its best client. The shop burns to the ground and the insurance doesn't cover it. We walk in on our spouse in bed with another. The burning anguish of life is often the way whereby we come to know God.

Out of the Ashes

Here lie the remains of what I thought I understood and knew. Here lie the sad remains of my feeble attempts to prepare for the inevitable injuries of the human soul. Here lie the tearstained hopes I had for quicker success, easier accomplishments, friends to celebrate with, and a marriage that would last forever. Here lie the ashes of what I had, what I had to lose, in order to lay hold of what God had in store next. This is the birthplace of faith. It is death, pure and simple, plain and clear, cut and dried. Out of the ashes rises faith.

There is an old saying: "Everybody wants to go to heaven, but no one wants to die." The truth of the matter is that death may be the only bus leaving for heaven, and if you want to go, sooner or later you just have to get on board. The old patriarchs ignored opportunities, purposely missing chances to escape the painful experience of death so that they might gain so much more than what they had by passing through the chilly waters of death.

> *Women received their dead raised to life again: and others were tortured, not accepting deliverance; that they might obtain a better resurrection.*

HEBREWS 11:35 (KJV)

Who wouldn't accept deliverance except someone who knew that death is only a means to a far greater end? We should all remember this. You must realize that your cross is the rod of your crown. What you have now may have to die to evolve into what it is going to be. Here I speak not merely of the death of loved ones but of promising careers and budding relationships. I speak of failure in business and the shattering of dreams. Expect to go through changes before you see the image the Master had in mind when He took the snapshot in your life and began the process. The negative dies and actually inverts to produce the radiance of the picture. If we are going to get to the next dimension of anything, what we now have may be the offering that it takes to get us there.

Sadly, some people hold on so tightly to what they have and never want to let go. Sure, these people do not lose, but they don't gain, either. This is the greatest mistake people make. They are so in love with their blessing of now that they choke to death the potential of tomorrow. When loss—an inevitable part of life—occurs, they get paralyzed in mourning, focusing so intently on what is gone that they completely miss what's coming. You have to be willing to see people leave, fortunes diminish, and plans fall flat, in order to move on and up. Things must die to be reborn to the next level.

The death of dreams is not the end of hopes. I want to share with you that there are better resurrections that have often come after the divorce is final. Am I for divorce? Absolutely not. But I am for survival. I do not believe in letting life kill me. There is life after disappointment. Like a couple who gets along better after the divorce than before. Like the professional whose career ends in total disaster, and who then discovers a new path in life that is more successful and fulfilling. In cases like these, one almost thanks God for what one went through to get to the next

> *Faith is to believe what you do not see; the reward of this faith is to see what you believe.*
> SAINT AUGUSTINE

level. Please, I am not suggesting that anyone ever really rejoices over the death of their child. Maybe not on this side of life, anyway. But funerals and all of their sadness will seem pointless in the resurrection. Likewise, when we get to the other side of trouble and see what develops out of the process of pain and despair, our faith gains dimension and depth.

Faith's Resurrection

So often God's integrity is placed on the line by our questions. Why did I have to go through this? Why did I lose this or that? God has to be extremely mature, beyond worrying about public relations, to stick to His plan and see it through in the face of criticism even from his fans. There are times that life takes turns that leave even the most faithful person staggering and reeling in the throes of agony and confusion. The word "why" keeps echoing from the pit of despair. It is during this time that we experience the end of our faith. Yes, that's right. There are limits to how far our faith can go. It is but human faith, fragile and temporal. Our faith fails sooner or later. And it must do so, for it is then that we reach the crossroads between greatness and mediocrity. It is there that we have the bar mitzvah of the spirit, that spiritual coming-of-age experience. It is when our weak faith evolves into a faith that was previously beyond our grasp.

> *There are many things that are essential to arriving at true peace of mind, and one of the most important is faith, which cannot be acquired without prayer.*
> JOHN WOODEN

Can we talk about the outer limits of faith—that is faith that has been stretched beyond its endurance by life's adversity? Yes, even faith-filled people experience moments when faith slows its beat and the monitor goes flat line and they are totally vulnerable. But God has the ability to resuscitate our faith. It is amazing how resilient faith is if cared for properly. It is on the other side of pain that faith returns in its newest and strongest dimension, having survived the unthinkable and outlived the impossible. Now faith refuses to be intimidated by anyone or anything. Faith often gets its diploma at the breaking stage of life.

If we are faithless, he will remain faithful, for he cannot disown himself.

2 TIMOTHY 2:13 (NIV)

186

The strength of this Scripture for the person of faith exists in the fact that Paul says "we" and not "they." "We" is inclusive. All of us, even those of us called believers, could be faithless. Yes, there are things that will happen to the faithful that will make them feel faithless. Here is Paul, the day after Pentecost, with an energized, miracle-working church, and he reminds them that in spite of the glowing experiences they have achieved, there will still be times that even "we" fit in the category of the faithless. What a liberating statement! It relieves the weight of pretending we never doubt and eases the guilt when we inevitably do. We all sometimes stumble in the dark and cannot see our way clear. Thank you, Paul, for releasing us from the pressure of trying to be perfect believers who never feel abandoned or betrayed, who never question God's judicious decisions that often override our petitions of faith. He is like a parent who must be able to teach His children to ask and yet be strong enough to decline the request when He knows that the end justifies the means!

But I am most excited about the comma between "faithless" and "he." It is this pause interjected by the translator that gives me a moment to reflect on the fact that between my faith's failure and His faith remaining is the death of the external that I might have the eternal. This pause, this comma, is to my faith what a phone booth is to Superman. It is the place where I change from my human, finite faith to His supernatural, divine faith. It is the stark and glaring difference between His faith and mine that I now want to discuss.

The Faithfulness of God

Oh, I have had my moments of faithful gallantry when I, with unshakable conviction, have maintained a steady grasp on the wheel while others capsized beneath the swelling current of adverse conditions. I have been known to be valiant in battle and stable in calamity, and I have seen the power of God do the unlikely and the almighty. Yet, if I am allowed total honesty, there have been times my faith has crashed and burned. My faith ultimately collapses at funerals, occasionally faints when my children are ill, runs from marital troubles, may avoid controversies with friends. So I can relate to the faithful and to the faithless, and I am thankful that even when we are faithless, God remains faithful.

I would suggest that God's faithfulness is painted more opulently when it is displayed on the canvass of our faithlessness. When we are at our best, we cannot determine by whose might we have achieved what we have accomplished. Occasionally, we need the experience of seeing how much can be done in spite of us rather than with us. My favorite hymn is "Great Is Thy Faithfulness." One could easily add this verse that I have written:

> *Great is my faithlessness yet thou art faithful.*
> *When I doubted you still brought me through.*
> *All I have needed your hands have provided.*
> *Great is thy faithfulness in spite of me.*
> *God is faithful when we are faithless.*

God told Thomas he was faithless (John 20:27). He told Peter he was of "little faith" (Matthew 14:30). Yet He was faithful to both men. Paul talks about transitioning from his human faith to divine faith. This is the faith that develops in the darkroom. It is the faith that comes from being through things that cause the candle of the soul to flicker. Yet in the midst of that flickering light, there remains a light that burns without a natural source or resource. It is the candle of the Lord, and it burns with us, often in spite of us. Sometimes when you have exhausted all of your resources, like the last two cylinders of an eight-cylinder car, His faith resumes the momentum when yours has expired. It is this faith that is invincible and quenches the fiery darts of wickedness and adversity.

Eternal Life

> *I am crucified with Christ: nevertheless I live; yet not I, but Christ liveth in me: and the life which I now live in the flesh I live by the faith of the Son of God, who loved me, and gave himself for me.*
>
> GALATIANS 2:20 (KJV)

We have talked about the things that crucify us, engulf us in darkness, and strip us of our frail faith. But we have not discussed how, in spite of all the pains and struggles, "nevertheless" we live. Isn't it amazing how you thought you were going to die, but you didn't? Have you ever thought you were going to break, but you somehow did not? This is the "nevertheless" of faith. It is the faith that comes at the extremity of our faith's reach. When our faith is extended and although fully stretched still falls short of being enough, God steps in and enables us to move into the realm of faith that is not normal. This is abnormal, supernatural faith. It is in you, but it is His faith.

If you are going to "live" by faith, life will occasionally hand you something that "you" cannot live with. It is at that moment that His faith continues where yours collapses. You suddenly realize that He carried you through the funeral. He carried you through the divorce, the sickness, or the trauma. It is His faith that we finally grow up into, not ours. I never knew about His faith as long as I had my own. It was the asphyxiation of mine that unearthed His faith. Of all places to find it, I found His faith in the darkroom, where with utter pain and no ray of hope to interrupt the process He tediously developed the picture I couldn't see. There in the darkroom, I transitioned from my faith to His and realized that without Him carrying us—even the strongest of us—we are frail and incomplete.

13.

Evidence That Demands a Verdict

The courtroom is in session. The room is hushed and the atmosphere is tense. The rumors have reached a crescendo suggesting that there is some valid and conclusive information that will be submitted by the district attorney—information that will unequivocally remove all doubt from the jury's mind as to the defendant's innocence or guilt. The defendant looks uncomfortable; the defense attorney has tried repeatedly not to allow the evidence to be submitted. Everyone knows that strong evidence can make a case. In fact, the case is no stronger than the evidence it rests upon.

Right in the middle of the proceedings, the district attorney makes his move: "Your Honor, I would like to submit article number 847321 as admissible evidence relative to this case." "I object," the defense cries out! "Overruled," says the judge in a matter-of-fact way. And as simple as that, irrefutable evidence will leave an indelible mark on the minds of those who are present. It is evidence that wields the sword of justice and steers the verdict one way or another. Based on this information, the jury will make its decision.

In a similar fashion, we are faced with compelling evidence that will require a decision to be rendered concerning the guilt or innocence charged against us by a lifetime of choices and actions, and our ultimate relationship to the Almighty Judge. In our case, though, the evidence that is most compelling cannot be seen. It is, rather, the evidence in the absence of tangibles. It is the evidence of our faith. Now we know that faith is according to Hebrews 11: "the evidence of things not seen." If faith is evidence, then it requires a verdict. No one submits evidence unless it is conclusive in nature.

> *For by grace are ye saved through faith; and that not of yourselves: it is the gift of God.*
> EPHESIANS 2:8 (KJV)

In this age of what I call "faith fanaticism," what will faith submit for the decision maker who needs concrete and conclusive evidence rather than suspended sentences and abstract ideas? I am glad you asked.

I see faith as an anchor for the soul. It refutes facts, scoffs at critics, and stands undaunted in the face of ridicule. Faith is the thing that enables the scientist to continue to look for a cure for a dreaded disease. He has faith that eventually he will find a concrete cure. That faith that he has may not be based on any facts, but it is nonetheless the fuel that moves him forward with abandonment and reckless commitment. If he were asked, "Are you a man of faith?" he might say, "No!" But that assertion would be incorrect. His effort is evidence that he has faith that he will eventually find a cure.

Faith is strong evidence. It is that assured knowing deep in one's soul that what is gestating as merely the seed of a thought will come through the birth canal of human experience and produce a flesh-and-blood nativity. But the strength of faith ultimately rests not on the assurance of our "knowing" but on the reliability of the One we know and choose to trust. It is the seed that He plants in our life that becomes the bedrock evidence that we can rest on even in the midst of condemning evidence submitted by our accuser. Ultimately, our faith must rest in the judicial fairness of the Supreme Judge. If we know and trust Him and His record in court, we can rest confident that even in the face of accusation and damning evidence, the ultimate verdict will be full of mercy and favor to us who believe.

Paul Makes His Case

In that consistent, stealthy way that he argues his case in most of his epistles, Paul approaches the bench of the theological with a rhetorical question. He says, "If God be for us who can be against us?" (Romans 8:31). This "if" that he raises seems unnecessary, as it is a foregone conclusion that God is for us, isn't it? It should be. Yet many who profess faith still do not really know that God is for them. They are somehow struggling feverishly to meet God's approval so that they can finally earn some meritorious badge of completion that wins them the favor of God.

I disagree vehemently. I believe that if our faith be in works, it is no more of faith. In other words, if I have to earn it, it is not faith. My works do not produce faith, but my faith will produce works. I cannot earn my way into faith. But having been the benefactor of faith, I will always have works that testify to the authenticity of my faith. Simply stated, if you believe it is going to rain you carry an umbrella. But know that carrying the umbrella is not what made it rain.

> For if Abraham was justified by works, he has something to boast about, but not before God. For what does the Scripture say? "Abraham believed God, and it was accounted to him for righteousness." Now to him who works, the wages are not counted as grace but as debt. But to him who does not work but believes on Him who justifies the ungodly, his faith is accounted for righteousness.
>
> ROMANS 4:2–5 (NKJV)

Back to this issue of "if" God be for us. Until that "if" is answered, our faith will be flawed. Until that "if" is answered, we will attempt to win Him rather than trust Him. Is God for us or not? Is he just for some of us? Who is the "us," anyway? The "us" mentioned here is the New Testament believer. Can we at least settle at this point the question that looms over the heads of many people of faith? Is God for us? Of course He is!

> He who did not spare His own Son, but delivered Him up for us all, how shall He not with Him also freely give us all things?
>
> ROMANS 8:32 (NKJV)

Paul submits the evidence of God's Son being crucified as evidence of the value God has placed on you. It is difficult to grasp that God—or anyone, for that matter—would offer up His only Son for the sake of another. But what defies all logic is that One would give up the Righteous Son for the ungodly one. Yet God, who needed to remove the "if" from your life, proved the immutability of his auspicious decision when he offered up his Son as a token of his commitment to me and you. In the face of such evidence, does it not then become increasingly difficult for the faith-filled to have doubts about the love and faithfulness of God toward us? This evidence of the cross is irrefutable evidence that God is for us. How can we look at the cross and then doubt what God thinks of us? How can we look at the bleeding drops of red running down the torn side of His youthful body and not walk away understanding that God proved his love to us once and for all with the price He paid to redeem us. If that fact ever becomes real to you, faith will erupt like a volcano. It is this evidence that enables the person who once had low self-esteem to reevaluate his or her own significance.

The Challenges of Faith

Paul having successfully proven that the cross is the greatest evidence of God's love for us, he then gives us five challenges in the face of this compelling evidence:

And we know that all things work together for good to those who love God, to those who are the called according to His purpose. For whom He foreknew, He also predestined to be conformed to the image of His Son, that He might be the firstborn among many brethren. Moreover whom He predestined, these He also called; whom He called, these He also justified; and whom He justified, these He also glorified. What then shall we say to these things? If God is for us, who can be against us? He who did not spare His own Son, but delivered Him up for us all, how shall He not with Him also freely give us all things? Who shall bring a charge against God's elect? It is God who justifies. Who is he who condemns? It is Christ who died, and furthermore is also risen, who is even at the right hand of God, who also makes intercession for us. Who shall separate us from the love of Christ? Shall tribulation, or distress, or persecution, or famine, or nakedness, or peril, or sword?

ROMANS 8:28–35 (NKJV)

1. What Shall We Say to These Things?

Romans 8:28–30 talks about God's Divine design. These lines say, in effect, that for those who love God, all things will work out in the end, for it is all predetermined by the Lord. Paul argues effectively that there is in fact a master plan that is orchestrated by an all-knowing God. He guarantees our future by determining our path. It's like God is the Director, but He doesn't film the movie of our life in sequence. Instead, it is shot in reverse; the ending is shot first and then all events occur to take us to that ending. It does not matter—come hell or high water, pleasure or pain, ridicule or adulation, the end is set.

What shall we say to these things? How can one expect to react to the news that no matter how bad things currently appear, they will all work out for the best in the end? If we are honest, we will admit it leaves us standing in a stunned silence. What a relief!

If we grasp the fullness of this knowledge, we really never have to doubt if we will survive, if we are on the right track, if we will make it. We can trust that God is for us and will never let us go astray. We can move ahead confident in our endeavors, secure in the knowledge that He has mapped out our lives and will lead us in the right direction.

2. Who Can Be Against Us?

This question does not deny the reality of opposition as much as it reinforces the outcome of the fight. When all is said and done, this question implies that whoever is foolish enough to fight the one whom God loves is predestined to lose. It trivializes your opposition and magnifies your support. It almost says, "Who dares to levy themselves against us in the light of such an arsenal of God's power and strength behind us?" The "who" that is against us is weighed against the power of the "God" that is for us. His favor has so much weight that he sways the case and tips the scales. It is like placing a brick on one side of a scale and a five-ton stone on the other. The brick has no chance of winning on a just scale when the weight of the stone is so much more than the rock of offense.

"Who can be against us?" also reminds us that the threat brought about by rumors, enemies, and assassins is thwarted by the bodyguard we have in the power and presence of God. It reminds us how ridiculous it is to be intimidated when you are armed by faith and its might. People who live by faith are often confronted with attacks and opposition just like everyone else, but they always arise victorious, often even when the enemy is more skilled than they are for the battle. This battle is not won by strength alone. The just live by faith. They fight by faith. They overcome by faith.

"Who can be against us?" is shouted out like a challenge that can only be heralded through a mouth that is totally convinced that God will always be with us. This challenge could not be made if God changed on a daily basis. There must be an element of security or it loses power and it becomes a real question rather than a strong challenge. But if you have faith, there is no opponent that can defeat you.

3. Who Dare Bring a Charge Against God's Elect?

Here Paul rips away the right to even raise an allegation against the elect. Oh, it is not that a charge could not be levied. God's elect are not perfect, just absolved, adjudicated by his sovereign grace. Who dare stand in the face of such a holy and all-seeing Judge and argue His decision? What evidence would they submit on any of us that He has not known? What compelling contribution could they add, considering that the one sitting on the bench is omniscient?

To be God's elect is to be one of the ones he has selected. The charge against an elected person is also a charge against the One who elected him or her in the first place. In essence, it is saying to the one who elected him, "You are wrong or misinformed." Now, history attests to the fact that we have elected officials and later found out information that made us seek to impeach them, but God elected us and He does not make mistakes. This is why

Paul argues in the very next phrase that it is God who justifies. When God makes the selection, who can question it?

Does not being able to bring charges against God's elect mean that we are prohibited from renouncing ungodliness and immorality? Of course not. But what it does warn us of is the danger of overstepping our bounds and going beyond identifying sin to renouncing individuals. Our message should always be one of reconciliation and not condemnation. If a brother is overtaken, our role is clear. We are commanded to restore him, not to attack him, discredit him, or humiliate him, or start a war against him or his country, or boycott his family. Do not

> *It is when all hope seems lost that the greatest faith is found. But every act in consequence of our faith strengthens our faith.*
>
> ANNA LETITIA
> BARBAULD

become anyone else's nightmare when you have your own. If not you, your children. If not your children, your parents. All of us need grace for forgiveness and faith for the future.

Fear of being charged falsely or even correctly by some accuser who threatens the demise of the believer is vanquished with this question. First of all, what man is worthy to judge another man's servant? How can you try a case that is out of your jurisdiction? The moment I expressed faith in Christ my case was moved beyond the lynch mobs of men to the just hands of God. The power of salvation is exhibited in the fact that my faith in Christ has placed me in God's jurisdiction and thus places me in the hands of a just God who has already handed in His verdict by indicting His Son on my behalf. Here we lay to rest the very attempt to lay a charge against God's elect. Whatever we are or are not, we are God's and His alone.

His verdict is against sin but not against the sinner. He has already executed Jesus Christ for my sins. Does that give me license to do wrong? Certainly not. It obligates me to do right— not under the threats of another weak and mortal man who has appointed himself as a vigilante of his brand of justice, but under a mandate of God's own goodness. I find myself face-to-face with such a love that it condemns my cheating heart to repentance. Faith wins the case before it ever comes to trial, as it has already armed the believer with confidence in the love and favor of God that causes him to live vicariously and victoriously through the victory of the risen Lord.

4. Who Is He That Condemns?

It is Christ who died, and furthermore is also risen, who is even at the right hand of God, who also makes intercession for us.

ROMANS 8:34 (NKJV)

Condemnation is now argued from the standpoint of His ability to have died for our past and to intercede for our future. The right-hand position is indicative of Him having God's ear on your behalf. What a privilege to consider that when you pray you are speaking to the Father through the Son who is seated at the right hand, the place of power and authority. It means that He is your representation. Your attorney is seated at the right hand of God. What a blessing! It is a proven fact that many people today find it difficult to find justice in the judicial system because they lack the finances to hire effective representation. This leaves them subject to justice based on the representation available. It is also true that even guilty people have been exonerated because they had excellent representation. Paul argues that you have the representation that causes you undoubtedly to win.

But this question is also an outright assault on the condemning voice of the accuser. It gets personal and counters the accuser with a question. The question is simply Who are you to condemn anyone? Paul argues: What gives you the right to judge and execute a sentence on me when you, if fully disclosed, could not live up to the scrutiny to which you subject others?

Oh, I know, you have no fear in that area. You have complete victory about this or that thing. But what about the other things that you struggle with every day? Are the only truly horrible sins the ones you don't practice? Even if you have gotten an A+ in perfect holiness, the challenge still remains; you have no right to condemn what you do not have authority over—namely, others!

God may judge you. He may chasten you. But He defies anyone else to correct His children. God reminds me of my mother, who had an ironclad rule that she explained to all of the neighbors in the community. It was very simple and very direct. She would tell you in a heartbeat: Don't put your hands on my kids. It wasn't eloquent or sophisticated, but oh, was it sincere! That is what God is saying to people who would think to condemn you. God says, "Keep your hands off of my kids!"

This fourth question prevents the frail human soul from drowning in the opinions of critics and succumbing to the vigilantes who often develop a posse to execute someone else. The mobs are threatening. It reminds me of the Wild West, where any group of angry men could be coerced into forming a mob and hanging a man without the slightest concern for true justice. These mobs are not of God. Sadly, we too often see this mob mentality in people who call themselves religious. The horrible, gut-wrenching fear of being tackled by these moral mobs who set themselves up as God's lynchmen is terrible. Religion, or should I say bad religion, has killed more people than has any-thing else in the world. There have been more Holy Wars than there were barroom brawls in the Old West. How can anyone pray for his own sins and then stone others for theirs? David said, "If you, O LORD, kept a record of sins, O LORD, who could stand?" (Psalms 130:3, NIV). Would you? I don't think so!

The condemning soul who condemns the believer fails to realize that God already knew his children's deepest weaknesses when he saved them. That is why Paul begins his discussion by teaching about God's great foreknowledge. Then he teaches that we are the elect of God. He explains that God knew who we were before He picked us. And who are you to impeach those He has elected? It is impossible for you to condemn what God has spoken up for. If that were possible, it would mean that the word of the accuser had more weight than the word of His own Son.

5. Who Shall Separate Us?

Now, the final question is "Who shall separate us?" And the answer is "No one," for faith rises up like a gladiator armed with strong steel that has been tempered by many trials. Faith stands up and wards off the ultimate fear: being severed from the peace of knowing who and what you are in Christ.

This fear is at the root of any fear you have, for what is there to be afraid of if God is with you? When you experience fear, you are not trusting that God is by your side to protect you; you are failing to remember that you are His child and He will not allow anyone or anything to harm you.

Now, all of us battle some sort of fear. Some wrestle the fear of being alone. Others are terrified of finding their spouse with someone else. The fear of growing old causes many to lie about their age and radically camouflage or alter their appearance, trying to hide the telltale signs of advancing years. Many live with a fear of heights. Your fear might not be the same as mine, but I guarantee you that all of us have something that makes us squirm.

Fear is one of the consequences of being human. Adam hid the moment he sinned. He was afraid of God.

> *Then the man and his wife heard the sound of the LORD God as he was walking in the garden in the cool of the day, and they hid from the LORD God among the trees of the garden. But the LORD God called to the man, "Where are you?" He answered, "I heard you in the garden, and I was afraid because I was naked; so I hid."*
>
> GENESIS 3:8–10 (NIV)

Adam says he was afraid so he hid. We often hide out of fear. We hide who we are, where we are, and how we are all because of fear. Fear of being rejected has forced many people into the bushes to cover themselves with fig leaves. It is easy to criticize someone else's fear when in reality we all battle with some sort of fear.

I have learned to combat my fear with faith. Whenever I am afraid, I remember that God is with me and will always protect me. I confess to you now that twenty-five years ago my greatest fear of ministry was the fear of living up to the expectations and scrutiny of others. I felt as if I was drafted into ministry against my will. I thought I wasn't worthy and was therefore afraid to say yes. I begged and pleaded with Him. Why would He even think about asking me to serve such a lofty position when He could have gotten anyone?

> *Faith is sometimes a means of survival. It is faith that gives you the courage to trust God when His will collides with your plans.*

At the time, I didn't realize that it was pride to have this fear. My fear questioned the way the Lord determined for me. My fear doubted His judgment. My fear didn't trust that He would always be by my side.

Faith is a powerful weapon against fear. I'm not saying that it is easy to combat your fears. No, you must destroy them one by one, day by day. Why, it wasn't until I was forty years old that I was able to overcome my fear of water. My sister nearly drowned as a child, and that inbred in me a fear that kept me at the shallow end of the pool. I would go to the beach, but I would go into the water only up to my midthigh. My wife, who shared this fear, would join me in the shallow water, where we would kneel and fake a swim; we'd swing our arms and laugh hysterically when the tide went back and we were exposed on our knees, stuck in the sand, not really swimming. It was fun and it was funny, but the truth of the matter is that behind the laughter there was a cold fear.

I finally tackled this phobia. Now I can swim all over the pool . . . as long as I'm on my stomach. Turn me over on my back and I am a little boy again, feeling out of control and insecure. You might be thinking, "How can you profess to have faith in God and still have this fear?" It is easy. I just don't lie. I do have faith, but it is human faith and sometimes it gets into a fierce battle with fear. Like everyone else, I need to remember that no one and no thing can ever separate me from my God. He will always be on my side.

> *For I am persuaded, that neither death, nor life, nor angels, nor principalities, nor powers, nor things present, nor things to come, Nor height, nor depth, nor any other creature, shall be able to separate us from the love of God, which is in Christ Jesus our Lord.*
>
> ROMANS 8:38–39 (KJV)

The final verdict has come in: Nothing is impossible to those whose faith fuels them by enabling them to feel the inner strength of being fortified by the invisible power of God. It is amazing that tangible obstacles can be moved by the intangible faith. Our faith is the evidence needed to change the verdict when life has handed us a death sentence. You do not have to accept every indictment that comes your way. The verdict cannot be entered into without faith being a factor. And as we are justified by our faith, the case has been already decided in our favor. The verdict is in. The jury has come back. Simply stated, the charges against us have been dropped. Even the guilty have been acquitted because of their faith in God. What does that mean? Due to extenuating circumstances—that is, God's mercy and grace—when all is said and done . . . WE WIN!

Final Words

Your reservations have been made, your ticket is in hand, and you are prepared for the next leg of the journey of life. You snake your way through the line of fellow travelers and approach the ticket counter. "How many bags do you have?" the attendant asks.

"Three" is your reply. "I've learned through my journey thus far to pack light and carry only those items that are crucial to my reaching my ultimate destination."

The attendant smiles. "You are very wise," she says matter-of-factly. "Many of your fellow travelers never make it to their destination. Some attempt to carry too much and find that they are unable to bear the strain and weight of bags they should have left home. Others find, upon check-in, that in their lack of planning, they brought bags they really didn't need and left some of great importance at home in the attic or closet. By the time the plane is ready for departure, it's too late to return and change bags."

"What a pity," you reply as you hoist your luggage onto the recessed space in the counter.

"What three bags are you checking?" she asks.

"Faith, family, and finance," you reply.

"Did you pack these bags yourself?" she asks again.

"Oh, most definitely. It took me some time, and many struggles, to decide what to invest in each bag, but believe me, though I struggled, and sweated, and often wondered if I would ever get them fully packed, I did it," you say with a wry smile on your face.

"Have these bags been in your possession at all times?" she asks.

You wince. You know the answer that is required for you to be allowed to check your luggage onto the plane. But you also know the truth: that for years you were not in possession of all three bags. There was the season when your family suffered when you became too focused on making money and advancing your career. And then there was the long stretch of time when you drifted from the faith of your childhood, because you were too interested in carrying bags that were stylish on the outside but empty on the inside.

You take a deep breath. "Miss," you say, "honestly, I have not always been in possession of these bags." You tell her of the years when you neglected one for the other, and how you almost lost the family bag due to abuse. "But," you quickly interject into your monologue, "I have all three now, and can tell you in detail what I have invested in each one."

The attendant stares at you for a few silent seconds, then affixes the small security check sticker on your ticket, tags your bags, and lugs and dumps them on the conveyor belt behind the counter. Turning to hand you your ticket, she looks you straight in the eyes and says, "You have them all now, and that is all that ultimately matters. Happy travels!"

Are you ready for the exciting journey that God has planned for the remaining years of your life? Have you packed the right bags, and invested in each the contents that will be needed for a lifelong, and ultimately eternal, journey? If not, you can begin today. Like the traveler in our story, sadly, many of us must honestly say that we have not been in possession of all three bags at all times in our lives. There were seasons of poverty in our finances, unrest and brokenness in our families, and aridity in our faith due to ignorance. For most of us, we failed to see the principle that permeates this book—that of the great investment. If you leave these pages and close this volume with only one message, let it be that you will commit to invest. Invest your cash in both earthly and Kingdom investments, invest in those family and friends closest to you, and most important, invest in your relationship to the Lord.

You may have missed many years and many opportunities to invest, but it is never too late to begin. You may have planted years of bad seed, and now stand alone in the middle of a vast field reaping an unwanted harvest of thistles, briars, and nettles, but with God it is never too late to turn and begin anew.

No, I cannot promise you that the field of thistles will disappear and be replaced by a sea of ruby-tinted poppies. You will need to deal with the fruit of your early plantings. You may need to take a machete and hack away at your credit-card debt until you clear the ground of your credit report and can plant some good seed. Yes, you may need to take a shovel to the ground of your relationships, uprooting the roots of bitterness and unforgiveness toward those closest to you. And yes, you will need to mow down your field of excuses and unbelief, and replace them with the good seed of faith toward God. God is able not only to forgive, redeem, and restore your broken life, but also to give you a plan to clean up your field and give you new seed to invest for future harvest.

Remember that God has a plan for you and is committed to work all things out to get you to your final destination in His will. He is able to take even the bad harvest and work it together for good.

Do you now understand my admonition to not get weighed down with too much baggage? I hope so! Faith, family, and finances is a threefold chord that is not easily broken. Put all the other bags you have used in past travels out in your next garage sale. It will be enough for you to carry the remaining three. Reassess what you have invested in each bag to date, and focus on a plan to invest for the greatest return for the remainder of your journey. Approach the ticket counter of life with confidence, hoist your bags onto the recessed space in the counter, and answer all questions honestly: "I have not always been in possession of these three bags, but I have all three now, and can tell you in detail what I have invested in each one."

"Great," I say to you, "you have them all now, and that is all that ultimately matters. Happy travels!"